SABBATH PAUSE

Theresa,

a friend and ally

Pause, Breathe ... Repeat

Terry J Clark

Terry Chapman

Sabbath
PAUSE

Seven Weeks of Daily Practices

CopperHouse

Editor: Ellen Turnbull
Cover and interior design: Verena Velten
Cover image: © Jelena Veskovic/iStockphoto
Pre-press production: Katherine Carlisle
Proofreader: Dianne Greenslade

Scripture quotations from the *New Revised Standard Version*, copyright 1983, Division of Christian Education of the National Council of the Churches of Christ in the United States of America. All rights reserved. Used by permission.

CopperHouse is an imprint of Wood Lake Publishing, Inc. Wood Lake Publishing acknowledges the financial support of the Government of Canada, through the Book

BNC CERTIFIED | **BIBLIOGRAPHIC DATA 2011-12**

Publishing Industry Development Program (BPIDP) for its publishing activities. Wood Lake Publishing also acknowledges the financial support of the Province of British Columbia through the Book Publishing Tax Credit.

At Wood Lake Publishing, we practise what we publish, being guided by a concern for fairness, justice, and equal opportunity in all of our relationships with employees and customers. Wood Lake Publishing is committed to caring for the environment and all creation. Wood Lake Publishing recycles, reuses, and encourages readers to do the same. Resources are printed on 100% post-consumer recycled paper and more environmentally friendly groundwood papers (newsprint), whenever possible. A percentage of all profit is donated to charitable organizations.

Library and Archives Canada Cataloguing in Publication
Chapman, Terry, 1955-
    Sabbath pause : seven weeks of daily meditations / Terry Chapman.

Includes bibliographical references.
ISBN 978-1-77064-445-8

    1. Sabbath--Meditations. 2. Time--Religious aspects--Christianity--Meditations. I. Title.

BV111.3.C43 2012   242'.2   C2012-903814-8

Published by CopperHouse
An imprint of Wood Lake Publishing Inc.
9590 Jim Bailey Road, Kelowna, BC, Canada, V4V 1R2
www.woodlakebooks.com
250.766.2778

Printing 10 9 8 7 6 5 4 3 2 1
Printed in Canada by
Houghton Boston

DEDICATION

*In memory of my mother, Jean, whose life and death
taught me about thin places
and*

*my father, Ray, who taught me the meaning of
sincerity and integrity.*

DREAM OF A WRITER IN EXILE

Mortal, can these bones live?

Ideas are scattered on the floor of

my study like dry bones in a wide valley.

It was you Divine One who sat me down

here among these bones.

Yet you ask me if they can live?

I want to put the question back on you

but cannot find the place in me

where such question lives.

Even deeper still resides the spark

that was born from the flint of your image.

Now in this dry valley, amidst the

rattling kindling of bones,

I blow on that shard of Presence as I hear my heart cry,

"O, Divine One, only you know."

Again you speak, this time in the imperative.

"Prophesy to the bones!"

I would prefer a Divine speech

(perhaps offered in the voice of James Earl Jones)

but, after a time of mustering courage, I yield.

"Okay, we can do this," and I watch as my small breath joins

creation's four winds.

Suddenly the chapters come together, idea to

idea, sinuous plot joining flesh of narrative holding

together the whole living story.

Even upon waking from the dream I am encouraged

by the promise and I begin once again:

Sabbath Pause Chapter One: The Beginning. . .

hoping you too, dear reader, are given to dreaming.

BASED ON EZEKIEL 37:1–14

TABLE OF CONTENTS

CONTENTS

IN GRATITUDE

Although *Sabbath Pause* invites one to a quiet, intimate centring in God's love, we all need people who can help us create a time and place in our lives that make the pause possible. My spouse, Dr. Jan Chapman, has been lovingly generous in this regard. Dr. Don Postema, my doctoral advisor, guided me in the early shaping of *Sabbath Pause*. I am grateful for my spiritual directors, and the congregations of Forked River and Roseland Presbyterian churches who have walked this path with me and contributed to its evolution. My friends at Heartland – The Convening Company, especially Craig Neal, have helped me go deeper into the Pause than I thought possible. The men's group I regularly meet with has helped keep me on the path. Finally, I wish to thank my editor, Ellen Turnbull, for her guidance that helped bring clarity to *Sabbath Pause*.

INTRODUCTION

*In the beginning when God created the heavens
and the earth...*
Then God said...and there was light.

*God saw everything that he had made, and indeed,
it was very good.*
*And there was evening and there was morning,
the sixth day.*

*Thus the heavens and the earth were finished,
and all their multitude.*
*And on the seventh day God finished the work
that he had done,*
*and he rested on the seventh day from all the work
that he had done.*
So God blessed the seventh day and hallowed it,

*because on it God rested from all the work
that he had done in creation.*

GENESIS 1:1, 3, 31 AND 2:1–3

THE BIBLICAL SABBATH – A DAY OF REST AND WORSHIP

SABBATH PAUSE – *A time and place in the heart of creation where we can receive the gift of a non-anxious presence and learn to live out of this essential blessing in service to the world. Practicing Sabbath takes us from the sometimes-cramped places of our lives to a place where our hearts can truly sing.*

We live in a world gone busy, in which an oft-heard complaint is that there just isn't enough time. We are busy doing so many things that we find it difficult to do just one thing intentionally. This busyness is not just a matter of not having enough time; it is a matter of not having an adequate framework for the time we have. This lack of foundation or reference contributes to lives that are fragmented and unsettled, and characteristic of the postmodern world.

Many thought that developing technologies would help humanity gain mastery not only over space, but time as well. We thought all the technology of the information age would "free up" time so that we could rest and play more. But just the opposite has happened. It seems that technology has given us more options to fill our time with, and not more freedom. We are not able to negotiate the challenges of time because we do not know how to truly rest.

The Judeo-Christian tradition of Sabbath can radically transform the way we live in time. It is a gift from God that can reestablish the rhythms of time and space that are more attuned to what God intends. The Jewish theologian, Abraham Heschel, who wrote a time-honoured book on the subject, gave us this beautiful definition of Sabbath.

Six days a week we wrestle with the world, wringing profit from the earth; on the Sabbath we especially care for the seed of eternity planted in the soul. The world has our hands, but our soul belongs to Someone Else. Six days a week we seek to dominate the world; on the seventh day we try to dominate the self.[1]

The biblical concept of Sabbath refers to a day, a 24-hour period set aside for worship, rest, and renewal. I believe this is a goal to aspire to. One can only imagine how the world would be transformed if we rested one day a week. But most of our lives are so far removed from this biblical concept of Sabbath that it seems foreign at best and may even bring up thoughts of legalism. Even Heschel acknowledges the difficulties of Sabbath-keeping, and writes, "In their illustrious fear of desecrating the spirit of the day, the ancient rabbis established a level of observance which is within the reach of exalted souls but not infrequently beyond the grasp of ordinary man." [2]

A child must learn to walk before she can run. This resource is intended as a step toward regularly practicing biblical Sabbath, a day set apart, "holy" unto God. During the seven-week program, we will build a bridge that spans the gulf between our hectic lives and the time-honoured tradition of Sabbath. This bridge will be built out of reason and narrative. You will read about the Sabbath in order to better understand its meaning, but you will also engage the language of the heart through story, metaphor, poetry, visual art, and music. Together we will explore rituals of transformation that may empower us to move from the chronological quagmire in which we are stuck to a spacious, simple, separate, and sacred Sabbath.

Please be open to how Sabbath practice unfolds for you. Each person's path is different. No one path is better than any other. If you focus on the ideas, metaphors, and experiences that gently open the self to God, this resource will help you learn to make Sabbath an integral part of your life.

The purpose of this resource is to help you grow through practicing and experiencing the daily prayers, reflections, and intentions. I highly recommend that *Sabbath Pause* be used in community, such as with a spiritual director or in a small group. On the seventh day of each week I have offered some guidance for how a group of Sabbath friends might gather and share their experiences from the prior six days.

Although these meditations are divided into days and weeks, please do not feel constrained to that pattern. You may wish to practice a particular breath prayer or intention for longer than a day before moving on. My prayer and desire is that you find a rhythm that works for you, one that heightens your awareness of God's presence in your life. Be patient with yourself. Let new insights, learnings, feelings, and promptings float lightly and luxuriously in your head and heart. Spiritual growth cannot be rushed. Prayer takes time to experiment with and practice. As Thomas Merton says,

> In the spiritual life there are no tricks and no shortcuts. One cannot begin to face the real difficulties of the life of prayer and meditation unless one is first perfectly content to be a beginner and really experience oneself as one who knows little or nothing, and has a desperate need to learn the bare rudiments. Those who think they know from the beginning never, in fact, come to know anything... We do not want to be beginners. But let us be convinced of the fact that we will never be anything else but beginners all our life.[3]

The New Testament concept of the Christian as a "sojourner"[4] conveys the sense of staying in a strange place only for a short time. We are reminded in scripture that this earth is not our native land. We are citizens of God's Kingdom. Sabbath practice moves us from here to there, to a place that is not far away, but just under the surface of our lives. May God's blessing be on you on the adventure of a lifetime.

PREPARING FOR SABBATH PRACTICE

Hanging on our dining room wall is a print of the Van Gogh painting "First Steps." It depicts a mother gently coaxing a child to take some tentative, awkward, life-changing steps into the waiting arms of the father, kneeling receptively across the garden. I invite you to take the following few "first steps" as you begin this seven-week journey of practicing Sabbath pause.

SLOWING DOWN

First, it is very helpful to slow down. Unless we learn to slow the pace of our lives, nothing will change for the better. When we slow down we have time to pray, to learn, to be together in community, and to heal. These are gifts that the pace of our lives buries. It is only in slowing down that they can be uncovered. When we pause, we remember that God's grace and love are present in our lives all the time, and that we are most alive when we are aware of God's presence.

I hope that pausing and slowing helps you to
>
> recall God's presence
>
> notice God's presence
>
> name God's presence
>
> deepen God's presence
>
> create a rhythm of prayer that enhances your awareness
> of God's presence.

A PLAN FOR DAILY PRAYER

The way you pray is as individual and unique as your relationship with God. As you begin to establish a Sabbath time in your life, notice what prayer styles emerge. What practices help you to focus or centre on God? You may want to close your eyes or watch a lighted candle, listen to music or sit in silence. Try to set aside time in the morning and evening and discern what feels the most comfortable. What time is best for you? Can you describe your prayer time?

A Gentle Reminder

Distractions, frustration, and/or fidgeting may occur often when you first begin to establish your Sabbath practice. God honours any attempts you initiate to recognize and communicate with the Divine Presence in your life. At first, try sitting and praying for three or four minutes at a time. This may be your first attempt to prepare your heart and mind for a holy experience. Be patient. Everyone has similar feelings at first. You may find that sharing your experiences with others provides some support.

Journalling

A journal can be a treasured companion and a vehicle to deeper spiritual awareness. Here are some guidelines for keeping a journal.

* Write with confidence and abandon.
* Others need never read your entries unless you choose to share them.
* Let your mind meander on paper.
* Nothing is insignificant.
* Trust your first impressions. They are usually the most authentic.
* Acknowledge any deeper feelings that come up of which you may not have been previously aware.
* Feel free to address your thoughts to God. Your address may be a salutation like, "God whose steadfast love and faithfulness never fails" or perhaps a lament or cry for help as in, "O God do you hear me?" It may help to imagine sitting with God over a cup of coffee and reflecting on the events of the day. The Psalms demonstrate a variety of ways one can authentically approach God.[1]
* Reflect on times and places where you've appreciated God's presence in your life.
* Use your journal for prayers of recollection.
* Return to your journal from time to time to recall how God was present in your experience.

WEEK 1

Beginning

In the beginning when God created the heavens and the earth.

GENESIS 1:1

HOLDING PLACES

Between the stream's source,
hidden in the thick woods
bubbling up from dark
underground wells,

and the sea
with its moon-coaxed tides
and vast anonymity
into which all streams flow,

there are Sabbath ponds:
sweet, safe, calm
holding places where
all kinds of life find refuge.

May the waters of
our life, streaming from
an unnamed Source,
find refuge in earth's ponds

where we know
we are loved and accepted
and can let the gentle
currents wash away the judgement.

In this tender bowl of compassion
all kinds of new life
take shape and are
carried downstream

bringing with them the
gospel that quenches
many a thirst in this
dry and weary land

before finally,
in one shimmering
moment, finding rest
in the consummate sea.

All streams flow to the lower
place of the sea.
This is the power of
humble gravity.

DAY ONE

Freedom

For freedom Christ has set us free.

GALATIANS 5:1

IN THE BEGINNING, God created out of divine freedom, not because God had to or because God should have but because God chose to. We are all created in God's image; we are meant to be free. We are also created to live in relationship with God. Living in communion with God gives us sacred bounds to our freedom, and we are most free when our relationship with God is respected and nurtured.

The story of Adam and Eve is the beginning of humankind's effort to redefine our divine freedom as autonomy and control. This was the risk that God took when creating us with a free will, albeit a necessary risk for a loving relationship. Adam, Eve and all their children grasped for more power, more control, and more stuff, which resulted not in freedom but in slavery. While freedom is meant to be like glue that holds love together, autonomy always separates, individuates, and isolates. Seen through the eyes of autonomy, God becomes the other and the human is left with the illusion that she is all alone, in control of her life, stranded in the centre of everything, trying to make sense of it all. This illusion of separation creates a gossamer veil of increasing loneliness. Thomas Merton describes the outcome: "From the root of this error comes all the sour leafage and fruitage of a life of self-examination, interminable problems and unending decisions, always making right choices, walking on the razor edge of an impossibly subtle ethic."[1]

The good news is that the longing for real freedom rooted in relationship with God remains a powerful force at the centre of our being. It is the part of us that reaches toward God.

> A rubber ball held under water submits. Once released, it springs to the surface; and the deeper it is held the more it strains to rise. The human spirit possesses natural buoyancy. It can be held down by enslavement to the senses, by acquisitiveness and ambition, by anger and violence, or by what the New Testament calls "cares." It can be held down, but its natural tendency remains dynamically oriented toward God. It can never be entirely satisfied until this upward impulse is allowed freedom. To eliminate the divine dimension is to inflict a distortion on one's personality that ultimately results in great harm.[2]

I invite you to allow the longing for the freedom that is deep inside you to rise to the surface and find expression.

Sabbath practice is about placing our attention on our relationship with God. As you begin your Sabbath practice, notice any sense of obligation that is part of your motivation to begin the journey (I really should try to pray more, read more, listen more, etc.). Obligations needn't feel burdensome: they can be opportunities for a renewed relationship with God. Begin to replace "I should" with "I can" in your thinking. "I can pray. I can be more of what God intends for me. With God's help, I can heighten my spiritual awareness."

In this spirit of opportunity, gently set aside any expectations for your practice. Authentic growth begins with a simple invitation from God to listen and become aware of God's presence in your life. Let your beginning be a simple "yes" to God's invitation. Begin where you are, not where you wish you were, and let your Sabbath journey with God take you where it will.

FOR REFLECTION

What words, images, and feelings do you associate with freedom defined by autonomy?

What words, images, and feelings do you associate with freedom rooted in relationship?

Spend a few moments now reflecting on the following poem about your true freedom.

KNOWING A SONG BY HEART

There is a song
Your heart knows.

An ancient melody
Easily forgotten

That you can hear
When you are still.

Your true freedom is
The sounding board

Which gives resonance
Echoing the vibrations

Now audible notes
That seem strangely familiar

As you begin to move
Once again on the path

With a new lightness in your step
And a whistling tune on your lips.

INTENTION

You are invited to name an intention for each day during this seven-week practice. This is a way to be mindful of your Sabbath practice throughout the day. You may want to write this intention on a sticky note to be placed where you will frequently encounter it, or set up an hourly reminder on your cellphone to look at it. The intention for this day is

INTENTION ***Today I pray for the Grace to be, to gently notice what is, and to be grateful for many kinds of freedoms that flow through my life.***

BREATH PRAYER

You are invited to breathe a prayer to God each day. With each inhalation, imagine you are taking in the breath or spirit of God. With every exhalation, imagine you are releasing a part of your spirit to God in prayer.

Saint Hildegard of Bingen, a 12th-century mystic, compared her life to a "feather on the breath of God." She also wrote, "The soul is a breath of living spirit that, with excellent sensitivity, permeates the entire body to give it life. Just so, the breath of the air makes the earth fruitful. Thus the air is the soul of the earth, moistening it, greening it."[3]

Try breathing this breath prayer over and over until it becomes part of you.

BREATHING IN *It is for freedom*

BREATHING OUT *Christ has set us free*

DAY TWO

Rhythm

The meaning of Sabbath is to celebrate time rather than space. Six days a week we live under the tyranny of things of space; on the Sabbath we try to become attuned to holiness in time. It is a day on which we are called upon to share in what is eternal in time, to turn from the results of creation to the mystery of creation; from the world of creation to the creation of the world.

ABRAHAM HESCHEL[4]

THERE IS NOT enough time! That seems to be a common cry of our leisure-starved culture. We hurry from one activity to the next. Breathless and exhausted, who can stop long enough to pray?

This "dis-ease" can be described as spiritual arrhythmia. Like an irregular heartbeat that causes fatigue, stress, and even death, our lives are out of synch. Chemical equilibrium can be restored with medication and life-style changes. Sabbath practice is the antidote for spiritual arrhythmia. Sabbath is an opportunity to reclaim our natural spiritual rhythm buried under layers of busyness, distraction, and clutter.

Often we extend all of our energy and resources trying to control our space. We like our space to be comfortable and filled with things that give us pleasure. We work many hours each day in order to accumulate more and more stuff (or if the stuff doesn't help, we may turn to food or drugs or work in the hope of being filled). But sooner or later, restless and unfulfilled, we become aware of the shallowness of materialism. We yearn to slow down and change our focus.

But most of us don't know how to begin to think and live differently. We have no map to lead us out of the gripping maze of materialism. Perhaps we procrastinate, thinking, the sooner I can retire the better! Then I'll have the time. One of these days I'm going to take a long vacation. But when we do retire and have free time, we fill it with activities. Then once again we have no time!

When it comes to having free time, however, we aren't quite as sure what to do. We spend so much of our energy on filling space that we dread unplanned time and become extremely uncomfortable when forced to look time in the face.

This tension between time and space causes spiritual arrhythmia. Sabbath is an opportunity to bring into balance time and space (which are intricately woven) so they are more in synch, and so that our life has a steady rhythm.

Sabbath is a rhythm that we can practice in our lives today. Vacations are refreshing; retreat days or weekends are restorative; retirement can be fulfilling. But we don't have to pursue our anxiety-filled lives or wait for some unknown future time to experience much-needed serenity and renewal. The little Sabbaths, the prayerful pauses along the way, will set our course of contentment. Now is the time to stop being controlled by the oppression of agendas and allow the gift of Sabbath to restore balance.

It is not a thing that lends significance to a moment; it is the moment that lends significance to things.[5]

> You can punch my lips so I can't blow my horn,
> but my fingers will find a piano.
> You can slam the piano lid on my fingers,
> but you can't stop by toes from tapping like a drum.
> You can stomp on my feet to keep my toes from tapping,
> but my heart will keep swinging in four-four time.
> You can even stop my heart from ticking,
> but the music of the saints shall never cease.
>
> GRAFFITI ON A NEW YORK CITY SUBWAY[6]

> *Rhythm is the soul of life. The whole universe revolves in rhythm.*
> *Everything and every human action revolve in rhythm.*
>
> BABATUNDE OLATUNJI[7]

FOR REFLECTION

Touch a part of your body where you can feel your pulse. Feel the rhythm; steady, constant.

Try to imagine the rhythm of your spiritual life. Is it steady or rushed; constant or erratic?

What kind of music do you like (jazz, country, classical, popular, Latin)? Can you describe how the rhythm of that music is mirrored in your life?

As you touch the rhythm of your life, can you imagine God dancing with you according to that rhythm?

INTENTION ***Today I am aware of the rhythm of Spirit in my life.***

Breath Prayer

BREATHING IN *A time to weep, and a time to laugh*

BREATHING OUT *a time to mourn, and a time to dance*

DAY THREE

Breath

Then the Lord God formed Adam from the dust of the ground, and breathed into his nostrils the breath of life; and Adam became a living being.

GENESIS 2:7

IN EXODUS 31 we read that *"God made the heaven and the earth but on the seventh day he ceased and paused for breath."* See? Even God paused for breath.

Breath is connected to rhythm. One way of telling if your life is out of synch is by noticing your breathing. My father was one whose life was somewhat emotionally and spiritually arrhythmic. He seemed to always struggle to discover a rhythm in his life. I could tell by his breathing when he was particularly out of sorts or stressed. He tightened his lips and forced out shallow breaths.

Breath can be like a relief valve on an air compressor. When the pressure builds up, the valve releases some air to prevent the tank from exploding. People who suffer from panic attacks often struggle to breathe. The short-term therapy is to breathe into a paper bag to automatically calm the breathing while the panic subsides.

Many of the great religious traditions, including Christianity, emphasize breathing as a way to begin prayer and meditation. The word for breath in both Hebrew and Greek is the same as the word for spirit and wind (Heb. *ruah* and Gr. *pneuma*). The Holy Spirit is the Breath of God that moves within us and enables us to know what we know of God and to feel what we feel of God. As Jesus puts it, the Spirit will continually remind us of what Jesus teaches (John 14:26). The language of breath and Spirit is the language of intimacy and immediacy. God is as close to us as our very breath. Breathing is our link to life and to the universe. Each inhalation and contraction of breath keeps us in balance. When we stop breathing, or breathe in a constricted way, fear grips us.

FOR REFLECTION

"Peace be with you. As the Father has sent me, so I send you." When he (Jesus) had said this, he breathed on them and said to them, "Receive the Holy Spirit" (John 20:21–22).

Breath reminds us that we are connected to God. Become aware of your breath.

Right now, take a minute to close your eyes and focus on your breathing.

Each time we take in breath and let it go, a cycle is completed. Right now, for one minute, notice how your breath flows gently in and out. Count each cycle without hurrying or altering your breath's natural rhythm.

How many times did your breath come in and go out? How did it feel to focus on counting your breaths? Did the minute pass quickly or slowly? Did time seem suspended?

There is great value in being conscious of your breath. It can make you aware that you are alive at this moment.

INTENTION *Throughout this day I notice my breathing. Each moment I spend in this way increases my awareness of the Spirit in my life.*

BREATH PRAYER

BREATHING IN *Breath of God*

BREATHING OUT *breathe on me*

DAY FOUR

Creativity

Now God saw all that he had made,
and it was exceedingly good!

GENESIS 1:31

WOODWORKING IS A passion of mine. I learned how to work with the tools of the trade in my first career as a carpenter. Once I worked on a crew in Texas that built a house every ten days. The pace of production did not leave room for precision or details. How different that was from my current hobby of making furniture. Furniture building is a craft that cannot be rushed. If I hurry, I am liable to measure wrong, gouge a piece of precious wood, or worst of all, injure myself.

My woodworking mirrors the creativity engendered by Sabbath. When I enter my woodshop I enter a different atmosphere. It is not a place of work. For me it is a Sabbath space.

Sabbath is about enjoying creation. Sabbath allows the time and space that are essential for creativity. The Sabbath pause and the flow of creativity are closely related.

The seventh day is like a palace in time with a kingdom for all.
It is not a date but an atmosphere. It is not a different state of
consciousness but a different climate. It is as if the appearance
of all things has somehow changed. The primary awareness

is of our being within the Sabbath rather than of the Sabbath being within us. We may not know whether our sentiments are noble, but the air of the day surrounds us like spring which spreads over the land without our aid or notice.[8]

God established a balance of creativity and rest and calls us to do the same. Sabbath is our invitation into a rhythm of prayer, study, reflection, and recreation, which are all necessary to nurture our true creativity. In that rhythm, we may freely respond to God's invitation.

Sabbath practice will allow the fullest expression of the Divine within us to unfold. As we open to the creative stream in which we wade, we begin to notice the thoughts and ideas that are floating all around, "concealed within the corporal surfaces of unlikely narrative" (this beautiful line from Isaac of Nineveh, 700 CE).

So we ask:

Where am I on the spiritual path that I imagine unfolding before me?

How am I living into the hope of a whole new creation that has already begun?

Where in me is the space being made for the new to be born?

How am I helping to create holding environments where creativity becomes a communal adventure?

What are the voices of resistance (judgment, cynicism, fear, etc.) that I keep listening to? What are they saying and why do I so easily believe them?

Something wants to be born. Pray for the grace to let the birth come in its own time, when you are ready, when you have lived these questions a little longer, when you are willing to be changed into fire.

Abba Lot came to Abba Joseph and said: Father, according as I am able, I keep my little rule, and my little fast, my prayer, meditation and contemplative silence; and, according as I am able, I strive to cleanse my heart of thoughts: now what more should I do? The elder rose up in reply and stretched out his hands to heaven, and his fingers became like ten lamps of fire. He said: Why not be changed into fire?[9]

FOR REFLECTION

How do you express your creativity?

What feelings do you have when you are enjoying your creative gifts?

INTENTION ***Today I explore and honour the creative gifts that reside within me, allowing them to find expression.***

BREATH PRAYER

BREATHING IN *In Christ, there is a new creation*

BREATHING OUT *everything has become new!*

(2 CORINTHIANS 5:17)

Cleaning House

*I will give them one heart, and put a new spirit
within them; I will remove the heart of stone from
their flesh and give them a heart of flesh.*

EZEKIEL 11:19

See, I am making all things new.

REVELATION 21:5

‹

I N THE CHURCH where I grew up, the emphasis was on being born-again. (Born again is a biblical term from John 3.) There was also emphasis on repentance, which for some meant, "Clean up your act!" However, as I read the scriptures it seems to me that rebirth and repentance each have two sides – God's and ours. Like the wind, the Spirit blows where it chooses. Rebirth is God's doing, and there is no telling when and where God's wind will blow through your life. Yet the scriptures teach that rebirth, renewal, and salvation are collaborative efforts. They are initiated by God through God's loving grace, and they are received and accepted by us. Our part is to receive the gift. This involves making room in our lives for God's gift of salvation. This may require some internal housekeeping.

Kathleen Norris tells a story of a boy she met while working as an artist in residence at a parochial school. She invited the children to write poems about God.

> Once a little boy wrote a poem called "The Monster Who Was Sorry." He began by admitting that he hates it when his father yells at him; his response in the poem is to throw his sister down the stairs, and then to wreck his room, and finally to wreck the whole town. The poem concludes: "Then I sit in my messy house and say to myself, I shouldn't have done all that." "My messy house" says it all: with more honesty than most adults could have managed, the boy created a metaphor for himself that admitted the depth of his rage and also gave himself a way out. If that boy had been a novice in the fourth-century monastic desert, his elders might have told him that he was well on the way toward repentance and not such a monster after all, but only human. If the house is messy, they might have said. "Why not clean it up, why not make it into a place where God might wish to dwell."[10]

Our inner space becomes cluttered too. Dust collects. The house can fall into disrepair. Sabbath is taking the time to prepare your inner space for God. Try to take some time today to make room for God. You will feel better!

FOR REFLECTION

Imagine your inner life as a room or house. What is it like?

Are there places you want to clean?

What is the quality of the light?

Are there windows or doors that you would like to open?

Attend to this inner housekeeping until you feel rested, more at home.

What is it like to invite Spirit into your fresh, renewed inner space?

INTENTION **Like relishing the feeling of living in a clean space, today I enjoy the fresh start that comes with each Sabbath pause.**

BREATH PRAYER

BREATHING IN *Create in me*

BREATHING OUT *a new heart, God*

DAY SIX

Review

O Lord our God, all this abundance that we have provided for building you a house for your holy name comes from your hand and is all your own. I know, my God, that you search the heart, and take pleasure in uprightness; in the uprightness of my heart I have freely offered all these things, and now I have seen your people who are present here, offering freely and joyously to you. O Lord, the God of Abraham Isaac, and Israel our ancestors, keep forever such purposes and thoughts in the hearts of your people, and direct their hearts toward you.

A PRAYER OF DAVID AT THE DEDICATION OF THE TEMPLE,

1 CHRONICLES 29

EARLIER, I NOTED that each of us develops a unique and personal style of praying. There are, however, many valuable lessons to be learned from those who have gone before us. A particular form of prayer that many have found helpful is the Prayer of Recollection, or *examen*. This prayer is an invitation to pause at the end of the day (or in this case at the end of the week) to look and review the week. It is like stopping along the road to look back at where you've been. It helps us to get our bearings for the next part of the journey.

So, pause and look back over the past week. Recall how God has been present in your life this week.

Notice the times when you were most aware of God's presence. Describe what the experience was like.

What rhythm of prayer have you found gratifying this week?

Have you been more aware of your breathing?

Early one morning during my Sabbath practice, I had an ordinary vision. I have titled it "Confession in the Shadows."

CONFESSION IN THE SHADOWS

From time to time it is a grace-full thing
to pause along the path, to turn from the light
and look behind to the shadow lands.
As I kneel on the path and turn in the direction
from whence I came I am silenced by the shadows.
They seem to stretch from the horizon.
Not darkness. Not light.
Not the most real thing, not an illusion.
Not separate from my form which cast them.
They are greed, fear, doubt, lust –
they are all there.
Resentment, impotence – they are all there
and many more variations hidden
in the shadows of muted gray tones
(it's no good running or pretending it's all light).
Clinging, they must always follow.

As I kneel and touch the cool path
I am reminded
by a grace-thrown voice
over my shoulder that it is good to notice…
After a Sabbath moment I rise slowly,
turn, and continue toward the light.
There is healing in noticing.
The backside once only dark has now been bathed in light.

INTENTION **Today I pause along the path to take a long, loving look at where I am**

BREATH PRAYER

BREATHING IN **Take me as I am**

BREATHING OUT **make me what I can be**

DAY SEVEN

Sabbath Group

A SUGGESTED GUIDELINE FOR SHARING IN THE SABBATH GROUP

(IF YOU ARE FOLLOWING THIS RESOURCE ON YOUR OWN, REFLECT ON THE QUESTIONS SILENTLY.)

How would you summarize what you have learned from your days of reflection on the theme of the past week? As you reflect, which day was

> your most restful?
>
> your most difficult?
>
> your most insightful?
>
> your most energizing?

Did any questions or concerns arise that you would like to bring to the group discussion?

Is there anything else that you would like to bring to the group discussion?

A NOTE ABOUT SHARING

Please be sure to listen to one another. Give every person ample time and opportunity to speak before anyone speaks twice. Remember that sharing time is not problem-solving time. The purpose of the gathering is not to take care of anyone's difficulties; rather, it is to listen to one another's spiritual growth by being present for one another.

OPENING PRAYER (TOGETHER)

*Loving creator God, you have made us in your image. We are in awe
of your beauty and majesty. Yet we are not always so sure of our own
beauty. Are you smiling on us as we begin our journey together? Are
you waiting for us in that quiet place of intimacy called Sabbath? Thank
you, God, for being so patient with us. We have become used to a way of
living that has squeezed you out in the same way that it has constricted
our own breath. Please be with us as we journey into this new land.
Guide us; shine your light on our path. We are ready to grow. Amen.*

Leader: Let us take the first steps on the road that God has established.

BREATH PRAYER (TOGETHER)

BREATHING IN *O Creator God*

BREATHING OUT *be our companion*

After two or three minutes of breathing the prayer together, the group
joins in the Taizé song "My soul is at rest."[11]

PRAYER

Leader: O Divine Life, guide and direct our time of sharing. May we listen attentively to one another as we remember your presence within us and among us.

People: Amen.

SHARING TIME

How do you feel about being made in God's image? Are there parts of your life that reflect this more than others?

What kind of music would you use to describe the rhythm of your life this week?

Does your inner rhythm differ from the rhythm of those around you (family, colleagues, friends, etc.)?

What kinds of play did you enjoy the most as a child?

What is one way you entered Sabbath time/space this week?

CLOSING
A Psalm
A Song of the Sabbath Day.
It is good to give thanks to the Lord,
to sing praises to your name, O Most High
(*breathe*);
to declare your steadfast love in the morning,
and your faithfulness by night
(*breathe*),
to the music of the lute and the harp,
to the melody of the lyre
(*breathe*).
For you, O Lord, have made me glad by your work;
at the works of your hands I sing for joy
(*breathe*).
How great are your works, O Lord!
Psalm 92:1–5a

GUIDED VISUALIZATION

Imagine that you are lying on the grass in a field surrounded by rolling hills. Feel the softness of the grass under your body, and smell the grass and the fragrance of the flowers around you. Look up at the sky above. Just be there.

Nearby there is a small country church. It has a bell that you can hear pealing. The bell's sound is both pure and joyful. It travels through the air and reaches you. It is your sound, a sound capable of evoking and stimulating your unknown, concealed joy.

Now you hear the bell again. This time its peal is louder. Feel its resonance within you. Realize that it is awakening your dormant possibilities. Then listen as it gradually fades, and be aware of the moment when sound ends and silence begins.

Once more, you hear the bell pealing. The sound is somehow closer to you, and you can feel it vibrating within you, in each one of your cells, in each one of your nerves. And at some moment, if only for a second, you become that sound – pure, boundless, vibrating.

Rest and rejoice in the attunement that connects you with the sound of God in the world.

BLESSING (TOGETHER)

Let us go in peace to love and serve the Lord. Amen.

Sabbath Is Spacious

*In the Beginning when God created the heavens
and the earth, the earth was a formless void and
darkness covered the face of the deep, while a wind
from God swept over the face of the waters.*

GENESIS 1:1

DAWNING OF A NEW DAY

*the day wanted to come
through the close opaque air
the silhouetted tree-line longed for depth
but the fog kept it to only two dimensions
while the geese and the ducks
seemed at home on the dreamy waters.
my soul wondered with me when
the mist would clear so I could
welcome the breaking day*

*that is how the Day will come –
not like peeling back a painting
from the canvas to reveal
what has been underneath all along*

but with the new Day light piercing the pigments
of all that is – burning, cleansing
rearranging the old to make all things new.

light even now shines through the life-scape
brilliance bedazzling now and then
when the hungry are fed
the aching listened to
the cast-out brought in
the nameless blessed
the weary given rest
the sleepers awakened . . .

my soul bids come away with me
through the incarnate fog
deeper into the liminal Sabbath –
smooth, watery, womb-like holding place
to be at home, like ducks and geese
who while waiting too glide freely
on water through a place once thick
now made thin by the encroaching light
revealing dimensions once hidden
*the new day at double trouble.**

*Double Trouble is the name of the state park where I begin each day
with a Sabbath walk.

Taking the Time for Sabbath

Be careful then how you live, not as unwise people
but as wise, making the most of the time.

EPHESIANS 5:15

IAN PITT-WATSON, my professor of preaching, used to say, "If you are looking for an illustration for a sermon, look at children." As I thought about the idea of taking time for Sabbath, I recalled an experience when my children, McKenzie and Nathaniel, ages five and two, taught me a valuable lesson.

The lesson in "Sabbath time" came one evening after 30 minutes of trying to persuade them that it was bedtime. My patience began to wear thin. It was late. I was tired. They were tired. We were cranky. As my frustration escalated, so did theirs. I was beside myself, which is a nice way of saying that I was acting from a place that did not represent my authentic self. Finally, in a sharp tone, I said, "Go to bed now! I don't have time for this!" Silence. Then McKenzie looked up at me and said, "Daddy, you don't like kids, do you?"

Much like the English language, the Greek of the New Testament has a wealth of terms to express the experience of time. There are three words that are used most often. *Chronos* means a point of time, a short span of time that is linear, orderly, and quantified. *Kairos* refers to the right moment, rhythmic and opportune. An *aeon* means a long period of time, or eternity.

Most of us live in allegiance to chronological time. The clock, by which chronological time is measured, makes us feel constantly rushed. Time is money, and money makes the world go round, and to the speedy belong the spoils. Of course there are deadlines to meet, kids to put to bed, jobs to be done, and a thousand and one other things to accomplish, so this is where we live most of the time. Sadly, it can drive us to places we would rather not be, and to actions we would rather not take, like blurting out, "I just don't have time for this!"

Hearing my daughter's response to those words surely took the wind out of my sails. I stopped in my tracks. Then I talked about my frustration and apologized for my outburst. We found ourselves in Nathaniel's room, he in the bed beside me and she nestled on my lap. There we sat for what must have been, although I'm not sure, a half-hour. It was a joy-filled, peace-washed time. Gratitude welled up from my heart as I thought about the precious gift of my children, and I offered prayers from that place in my heart. God be with us. God was. God is.

Sabbath creates *kairos*. When I sat with my children in the darkness of my son's room, the three of us entered a Sabbath time. The quality of time changed from a frustrated, stressed-out chronological quagmire to graceful, renewing, pleasurable, *kairotic* time.

And something else happened too. It was as if we entered, however momentarily, into a place of *aeon*. The ineffable presence of the Holy filled the room. It was awesome. It was prayer.

So what initially motivates us to "take the time"? For me, it was the crisis with my children. Other crises such as sickness, loss, and fear can move us to a *kairotic* moment, an opportune time. (Conversely, they can also move us deeper into the throes of chronological time. When pressured, we may be more driven by busy-ness. Through denial, we may move deeper into the control of *chronos*.)

Another motivating factor here to "take time" may be desire or hunger for God. It has been said "A soul cannot be cultivated in a hurry." When we get caught up in stress-filled times we can lose our direction and rhythm. Priorities become scrambled. Life feels out of control.

But there is yet another way, apart from crisis and hunger, to move from *chronos* to *kairos* to becoming more aware of a deeper reality, *aeon*. That way is to practice Sabbath, the intentional, regular, rhythmic time set apart not to do, but to be. And we don't have to retreat to a monastery to cultivate a Spirit-filled life. Practicing Sabbath allows us to find moments in our day for meditative thinking, praying, silence, and listening.

Practicing Sabbath creates opportunities for graceful transformation. Sabbath moves us from quantified time measured by clock and calendar to time measured only by God's loving presence. Someone once gave me a "Peanuts" cartoon in which Charlie Brown was complaining to Lucy that life was passing by too fast. (Sound familiar?) Dr. Lucy's response was, "Try slowing down around the corners." Sabbath allows us to put the brakes on around the corners. And that's where God always meets us – in the slowing. Then everything changes. It's a lesson my children taught me, just in time.

FOR REFLECTION

Time lost is time in which we have failed to live a fully human life, gain experience, learn, create, enjoy, and suffer. It is time that has not been filled up but left empty.

Dietrich Bonhoeffer[1]

William James once wrote, "My experience is what I agree to attend to."[2]
As you sit in your Sabbath space what do you see around you? Relax
and breathe deeply several times. Now draw your attention to your
inner world.

What do you see there?

What calls for your attention?

What is it like to pay attention to these things?

Today, try to be aware of the quality of your time. At the end of the day
note without judgment when you experienced

chronos: a point of time, a short span of time, linear, orderly, quantified;

kairos: the right moment, opportune time, rhythmic;

aeon: a long period of time, or eternity.

INTENTION ***Today I notice the different rhythms of "time" in my life.***

BREATH PRAYER

BREATHING IN *This is the day the Lord has made*

BREATHING OUT *I will rejoice and be glad in it*

PSALM 118:4

DAY TWO

Emptiness

"Go out and stand on the mountain before the Lord, for the Lord is about to pass by." Now there was a great wind, so strong that it was splitting mountains and breaking rocks in pieces before the Lord, but the Lord was not in the wind; and after the wind an earthquake, but the Lord was not in the earthquake; and after the earthquake a fire, but the Lord was not in the fire; and after the fire a sound of sheer silence.

I KINGS 19:11–13 – THE LORD'S WORDS TO THE PROPHET ELIJAH

C. S. LEWIS noted, "The further up and the further in you go, the bigger everything gets. The inside is larger than the outside."[3] When we begin to explore the depths of our lives, we first encounter all the things that fill our lives yet leave us unsatisfied. We're accustomed to being full, but long to be fulfilled. From our schedules to our stomachs, throughout our lives we are taught that we should never be wanting. Practicing Sabbath leads us to a deeper, bigger place, beyond the things like work and ice cream that fill the voids on the surface of our lives. The spaciousness of this place may seem like emptiness at first. It can be scary.

I found it challenging to approach this day of reflection on the emptiness of Sabbath. Thinking and writing about emptiness means experiencing it, for it is never far away. Very reluctantly, I am making friends with the emptiness that I often experience when I "take the time" for Sabbath. I am discovering that I have a choice. Either I embrace the emptiness and become acquainted with it, or deny it and turn away. Choosing the former, I am slowly being introduced to this friend – emptiness – as I plumb its depths and explore its cavernous spaces.

Because Sabbath time is so spacious and free and we are accustomed to the opposite, we experience the unfamiliar as discomfort. It often feels like a feared black hole. It is essential for the Sabbath sojourner to know from the start that Sabbath moments are not always pleasant. In fact, Sabbath can be uncomfortable to say the least. This discomfort may range from an annoying restlessness to feelings of guilt to momentary panic. Surprised and disconcerted by this, many people quit their practice at this point. Their discomfort may feel intolerable and they decide that Sabbath is not for them. This unfamiliar and uncomfortable feeling is not easy to overcome because often space is associated with fear, emptiness with negativity, and lack of fulfillment with dysfunction. It takes time, courage, and trust to learn to grow into spaciousness. As you practice Sabbath, you begin to understand that what feels like emptiness is not really empty, but a space full of grace and opportunity. Know that God's presence is with you.

Gerald May invites us to consider the 17th-century philosopher Benedict de Spinoza who said, "Nature abhors a vacuum."

Modern science has shown he was wrong. There is far more space than stuff in the universe. The atoms that make up all matter, including our own bodies, consist of vast distances of space between tiny subatomic particles. No matter how solid we may feel, we are much more space than substance. If any nature abhors a vacuum, it is human nature and that is only because our nature has been so adulterated by conditioning.[4]

FOR REFLECTION

(The Hebrew letters represent the name of God given to Moses in Exodus 3:14.)

WHERE THE WIND BLOWS

The wind blows
in one ear and
out the other.
But there is a
naming breath
in between.

הָוֹהִי

Into one ear flows
the sound of longing,
a tender whisper,
"come away
with me into
the desert place."

הָוֹהִי

Out the other
is heard
insatiable thirsting,
unconsummated longing,
the sounds
of silence.

הָוֹהִי

*When I hear
the name on
my lips my
ears wish my head
was missing...
Ahhhh...*

הָוֹהִי

*Into the empty
space between
my ears a standing
ovation rises as
longing and consummation
kiss each other.*

הָוֹהִי

Right now, give yourself a little space by taking a moment to sit; just be. See and hear what is around you and notice what happens within you. The restlessness or the discomfort that may accompany this spacious moment may be an invitation to stay and experience God's presence. Just as it takes time for our eyes to adjust when we move from darkness into light, so it takes time for our inner selves to adjust as we move from busy, driven-filled time into spacious-free time. Be gentle with yourself. Try to stay with God to explore what you feel and experience.

Let the rhythm of Sabbath carry you deeper and closer to God. Where is God in these spacious moments?

What may God be saying to you?

INTENTION ***Today I gently explore my depths as God lights my way.***

Breath Prayer

BREATHING IN *God fills the depths of my heart*

BREATHING OUT *with abundant love*

DAY THREE

Nearness: Sabbath Is Closer Than We Think

The Lord is near to the brokenhearted,

and saves the crushed in spirit.

PSALM 34:18

HAVE YOU EVER experienced the holiness of place? For two years I served as a pastor of a 900-year-old Scottish kirk. It was the church in which Robert Lewis Stevenson spent much of his childhood and where his grandfather Lewis Balfour was the minister. I experienced this church as a holy place. Something about its history and architecture engendered a heightened sense of nearness of the Spirit.

While in Great Britain, my wife, Jan, and I visited the Tower of London. Part prison, part fortress, it oozes fascinating history. The oldest part of this auspicious structure is the White Tower built by William the Conqueror in the 11th century. Housed on the second floor of the Tower is a small chapel named the Chapel of Saint John. It is built entirely of stone with a vaulted ceiling supported by 12 pillars. It was used by the Knights of the Order of Bath to keep an all-night vigil over their armour before the King anointed them on coronation day. Except for the light that shines through the arched windows, the chapel is empty. It is very silent, very still. To me, this is a Sabbath place. The reverent prayers from over a thousand years of visitors to this holy place can almost be inhaled as the sacredness of the place fills one's soul.

Just below the Chapel of Saint John is the most appalling of all the Tower's dungeons. Measuring four feet square by four feet high, it is impossible to stand upright or lie down full length in it. This stifling, cramped place is called Little Ease.

I remembered reading what Fred Beuchner said about this place.[5] He suggested that we are that White Tower. How much of our lives do we spend in the place of Little Ease when the Chapel of Saint John is so close and inviting?

Howard Rice's description of the spiritual life reminds me of the Knights in the Chapel of Saint John: "To be spiritual is to take seriously our consciousness of God's presence and to live in such a way that the presence of God is central to all that we do."[6] I can imagine how the Knights experienced a sense of holiness as they kept their vigil in anticipation of the coronation.

The word piety traditionally describes the vigilance of the spiritual life. However, most contemporary Christians have a negative reaction to thoughts of piety. It smacks of judgmentalism or self-righteousness. The fear of being too religious leads many to feel that things of the spirit are not for them. This fear reminds me of the place called Little Ease. Attitudes that restrict and stifle spiritual growth can be like dungeons in the soul. It is a place where, bound to outdated and worn-out beliefs, we simply cannot grow.

Sabbath space is like the Chapel of Saint John. It is there in you just on the other side of the wall that you have built up with fear, doubt, or disappointment. Go ahead; enter that space and be bathed in the light of grace and love.

FOR REFLECTION

LITTLE EASE

Two rooms make up this place
a preference as you'll see
One open to God's shining face
the other only room for me

There is much light in the one above
its windows wide and free
The one below but dampens love
there I sit to a tolerable degree

One's like the future grand with awe
the other sure and certain
One contained in canon law
the other lit through torn curtain

Why there are two I cannot know
but still a greater question
Is why I linger down below
in days of linear progression

A mystery though – there is no door
to keep me in this room below
Perpetually I have privilege of the floor
to live the truth I surely know

I've come of late to the light-filled space
and found my truer self there
Yet I strain against Love's embrace
its penetration too much to bear

So soon I find my home again
in the place of little ease
But the memory of light's domain
blows through like morn's fresh breeze.

Can you recall a time when you visited a place where you sensed the Holy? Perhaps an experience in nature, an old church, a family dinner, or some other gathering comes to mind.

Imagine a place in you that reminds you of that place.

Describe that space in you. Is it well lit or dim, spacious or small, warm or cold? What colours are there? Explore the height and width of the space.

Consider this verse from Psalm 139: "For it was you who formed my inward parts."

INTENTION **Today I am aware of the Holy Place that is in me.**

BREATH PRAYER

BREATHING IN *O Lord, I love the house in which I dwell*

BREATHING OUT *and the place where your glory abides*

(PSALM 26:8)

You Are Accepted

God saw everything that he had made, and indeed,
it was very good.

GENESIS 2:31

But now thus says the Lord, he who created you,
O Jacob, he who formed you, O Israel: "Do not fear,
for I have redeemed you; I have called you by name,
you are mine. Because you are precious in my sight,
and honored, and I love you."

ISAIAH 43:1, 4

I WAS INTRODUCED TO the work of Paul Tillich about fifteen years ago when I was in the throes of a painful divorce. My therapist suggested I read Tillich's sermon, "You Are Accepted." Tillich's message of God's unconditional acceptance was comforting and timely, a much-needed light in my darkness. The sermon contains one of the most poignant descriptions of grace I have ever read.

> Sometimes at that moment (of acceptance) a wave of light breaks into our darkness, and it is as though a voice were saying. "You are accepted." You are accepted, accepted by that which is greater than you, and the name of which you do not know. Do not ask for the name now; perhaps you will find it later. Do not try to do anything now; perhaps later you will do much. Do not seek for anything; do not perform anything; do not intend anything. Simply accept the fact that you are accepted. If that happens to us, we experience grace. After that experience we may not be better than before, and we may not believe more than before. But everything is transformed.[7]

Yes, I had heard the words of acceptance before. Yes, I had experienced God's unconditional love and unmerited grace. Yet Tillich's thoughts birthed a paradigm shift that continues to evolve for me. There are two aspects of my looking at and relating to God that were affected by this shift. I describe these as direction and response.

Where does God come from? When I am touched by grace, where does it come from? Tillich, with unmatched clarity, says that this grace comes from the Ground of Being. I had always thought of God as outside of me, the Holy Other. The idea of the transcendence of God far outweighed any thought or experience of immediacy. But for the first time I had the sense that God, while transcendent, was also present in the deepest parts of my being. I describe this as a directional change, a reaching in (rather than out) to experience God.

My perception of the response elicited by grace has also changed. When I read, "Simply accept the fact that you are accepted!" I was freed from the arid moralizing that plagued my previous thinking. The force of God's grace voiced in the simple indicative, "You are accepted!" took its rightful place before the moral imperative, "Clean up your act!"

Being precedes and empowers doing. With this spiritual shift I realized a transformative power and the renewed courage to follow God's call for my life.

Sabbath is a safe and sacred time and place where you can appreciate who you are. The Gospel is: You are accepted by God! As you continue to practice Sabbath, this amazing, powerful confession of faith will become a part of your living, breathing reality. You will begin to see God as the ground of your being rather than only as an object of veneration or religious tradition. Sabbath is a journey into the transforming love and acceptance of God that lies at the very centre of your being.

FOR REFLECTION

PEEL OFF BEFORE OPERATING
(The words on the thin protective plastic sheet covering most new appliances.)

There is a thin layer
over the surface of my life;
in fact there are many.
I did not come this way
from the factory.
The layers have been
added over time.

Some settled over years
like dust on the window sill.
Others were added quickly to protect
what lies beneath from
life's inevitable smudges.

More layers were accumulated
as projections of
others' expectations.

Beneath the egoic layers:
father, husband, pastor,
creator, writer, controller,
lies the essential me
who just wants to be loved
and love in return.
Now peeling away the layers
I am love in the hands of Love.

INTENTION **Today I will be more aware of the Holy Place that is in me.**

BREATH PRAYER

BREATHING IN *Take me as I am*

BREATHING OUT *shape me into what I can be*

Sabbath Guides

*I will lead the blind by a road they do not know,
by paths they have not known I will guide them.
I will turn the darkness before them into light,
the rough places into level ground. These are the
things I will do, and I will not forsake them.*

ISAIAH 42:16

LAKE KABETOGEMA, with its hundreds of miles of shoreline, is one of Minnesota's largest lakes. Just one of the thousands of lakes in the state's vast northern wilderness called the Boundary Waters, it stretches for what seems like forever.

Several years ago I was visiting a friend who owns a cabin on the lake. Don woke me before dawn for our excursion in his outboard. We cruised all day in the same direction and never got to the end of the lake. From time to time we would stop on a pristine island to swim, eat lunch, play, and pray. Never before have I had such a sense of vastness. The expansive spaciousness of this wilderness was breathtaking (or perhaps breath-giving).

As I sat on an island with only the sounds of the loons, the breeze, and the water lapping the rocky shore, I wondered, "What if Don left me here?" Conflicting feelings accompanied that thought. I felt fear at the idea of being left alone in that boundless wild place. Yet I also felt certain that Don would not leave me. Gratitude for his friendship and wilderness savvy settled into my heart.

An old African proverb reminds us, "It is because one antelope will blow dust from the other's eye that the two antelopes walk together." Know this as you continue on your Sabbath Journey: You are not alone. The Scriptures make this point over and over again. When God told Moses to go to Pharaoh and tell him, "Let my people go!" God also reminded Moses that he would not be alone. Two words were all that God needed to say. "I am." When we look at these words in their original language and context, they mean, "I am the one who will be with you, to guide you, to empower you, to deliver you, to accomplish my will through you." The frightened disciples, faced with an uncertain future and the immediate crucifixion of their beloved leader heard similar words. "When the Spirit of truth comes, he will guide you into all the truth" (John 16:13).

It is essential that we are certain we have the Spirit to guide us. We are guided by Holy Scriptures, the traditions and teachings of the church, and trusted friends who, like Don, are experienced in things of the wilderness. We can learn much from these friends. Do you have such a person in your life with whom you share your faith and doubts, hopes and fears? Such friends can lead you deeper into your Sabbath place and support you through any troubling aspects. Now is the time on your journey to make sure you have a guide or guides. Start by praying that God will lead you to such a person or group. Ask your pastor how you can be connected to a group or a soul friend. Find out what groups are meeting in your church. This is a huge step for many "rugged individuals" who are used to making their own way. So be courageous. Be intentional. Be comforted. Friends will make the way so much clearer.

FOR REFLECTION

Are you used to going-it-alone?

Can you sense God's Spirit accompanying you on the journey?

Recall times when you shared your deepest feelings with God or a trusted friend.

Read the following verses from John 14 slowly and prayerfully. ·

> "I will not leave you orphaned; I am coming to you. In a little while the world will no longer see me, but you will see me; because I live, you also will live. On that day you will know that I am in my Father, and you in me, and I in you. They who have my commandments and keep them are those who love me; and those who love me will be loved by my Father, and I will love them and reveal myself to them." Judas (not Iscariot) said to him, "Lord, how is it that you will reveal yourself to us, and not the world?" Jesus answered him, "Those who love me will keep my word, and my Father will love them, and we will come to them and make our home with them. Whoever does not love me does not keep my words; and the word that you hear is not mine, but is from the Father who sent me. I have said these things to you while I am still with you. But the Advocate, the Holy Spirit, whom the Father will send in my name, will teach you everything, and remind you of all that I have said to you. Peace I leave with you; my peace I give to you. I do not give to you as the world gives. Do not let your hearts be troubled, and do not let them be afraid."

INTENTION ***Today I bask in the warmth of God's acceptance.***

BREATH PRAYER

BREATHING IN *With God*

BREATHING OUT *I am never alone*

DAY SIX

Review

THIS WEEK WE entered into what for some is a new and unfamiliar territory. We began the week looking at the quality of our time and were invited to pause from the hectic pace of our lives and enter a more spacious, opportune time. We learned that this spacious time might feel empty and scary at first. But once our "eyes" adjust to this new place and time, we discover that God is close. In God's presence we learn more about ourselves. We begin to experience the reality of Emmanuel, God with us, in us, loving us. In this spacious place and time, bathed in God's light, we learn that we can also love ourselves. Not only do we have the assurance of God's presence, we are invited to share the journey with others who can guide us along the way.

UPON DISCOVERING NEW FRIENDS

I heard a rustling
in the tall grass
that surrounds
the bush behind
which "I" found cover.

Held breath,
tightened muscles,
heightened senses,
what new
threat approached?

A broken twig
more movement
and then a whisper
"I see you..."
"I SEE YOU..."

When I opened
my eyes I
breathed a sigh
of relief and
read a poem

to my
new friends
who sat around
the circle
built of trust.

FOR REFLECTION

Place a bowl of water before you. Think about how you spent your time this week. Imagine that this water is the week you just lived.

Now hold some water in your hand. How does it feel?

Are you gently holding the water or does it run freely through your fingers?

What do you want to say to God about this?

Have you experienced a feeling of emptiness this week? What was it like?

Were you able to stay with it? Did you fill it with something?

Have you invited another person to accompany you on your spiritual journey?

INTENTION **Today I savour each crumb, treasuring the taste of life.**

BREATH PRAYER

BREATHING IN *I have all the time I need*

BREATHING OUT *to truly live*

DAY SEVEN
Sabbath Group

OPENING PRAYER (TOGETHER)

Creating God, who brought us into this world, breathed your Spirit into us, and formed us in your likeness, we give you thanks for the strong cords of love that bind us to you and nourish us in this community you have created. We pray for your continued presence as we practice Sabbath.

Leader: This week we have gone deeper into the spacious dwelling of God who is with us and in us. Today we are reminded that we are not alone on this journey but share in community.

BREATH PRAYER (TOGETHER)

BREATHING IN *How lovely is your dwelling place*

BREATHING OUT *O Lord of hosts*

After two or three minutes of silence, the group joins in the Taizé song "My Peace I Leave You."

SHARING TIME

Describe one time this week when you felt stuck in the mud of **chronos**. What was the quality of that time?

Describe one time when you felt God's gift of **kairos**. What was the quality of that time?

Can you recall what it was (crisis, desire, choice, guilt, etc.) that moved you into Sabbath time?

A GROUP SPIRITUAL EXERCISE: *LECTIO DIVINA*

Lectio divina is an ancient way of praying with scripture that involves four steps: *lectio* (read), *meditatio* (ruminate), *oratio* (pray), *contemplatio* (rest). Begin this practice with a prayer asking for the Spirit to bring light to a chosen passage so that you may receive from it whatever God has for you. Invite someone in the group to read (*lectio*) the passage very slowly as each person listens for a word, phrase, or image that draws their attention or shimmers for them. Individuals may then be invited to share what came to their attention without elaboration.

After a few moments, the group is invited to hear the passage again, after which time is spend ruminating (*meditatio*) on the particular word, phrase, or image that surfaced. After some time, individuals may want to share a slightly fuller description of their experience.

The passage is read for the third time, followed by a more extended period of silence, during which individuals engage in prayerful conversation (*oratio*) with God about their experience with the word, image, or phrase that rose out of the reading of the scripture.

After some moments, the passage is read for the last time and followed by a period of quiet during which individuals are invited to rest (*contemplatio*) in the grace that has been given them.

Closing (Use this Psalm as a *lectio divina* exercise.)

How lovely is your dwelling place,
O Lord of hosts!

My Soul longs, indeed it faints
for the courts of the Lord;
my heart and my flesh sing for joy
to the living God.

Even the sparrow finds a home,
and the swallow a nest for herself,
where she may lay her young,
at your altars, O Lord of hosts,
my King and my God.

Happy are those who live in your house
ever singing your praise.
Happy are those whose strength is in you,
In whose heart are the highways to Zion.

As they go through the valley of Baca
they make it a place of springs;
the early rain also covers it with pools.

They go from strength to strength;
the God of gods will be seen in Zion.

O Lord God of hosts, hear my prayer;
give ear, O God of Jacob!

Behold our shield, O God;
look on the face of your anointed.

For a day in your courts is better
than a thousand elsewhere. I would rather be a
doorkeeper in the house of my
God than live in the tents of wickedness.

For the Lord God is a sun and shield;
he bestows favour and honour.
No good thing does the Lord withhold
from those who walk uprightly.

O Lord of hosts,
happy is everyone who trusts in you.

PSALM 84

After the *lectio* exercise, the group sings "Spirit of the Living God."[8]

BLESSING (TOGETHER)

The Lord is near. Let us not worry about anything but in everything by prayer and supplication with thanksgiving let our requests be made known to God. And the peace of God, which surpasses all understanding, will guard our hearts and our minds in Christ Jesus. Amen. (Philippians 4:5–7)

WEEK 3

Sabbath Is Separate

God said: Let there be light. God saw the light: that it was good. God separated the light from the darkness.

GENESIS 1:3–4

In the tempestuous ocean of time and toil there are islands of stillness where we may enter a harbor and reclaim our dignity. The island is the seventh day, the Sabbath, a day of detachment from things, instruments and practical affairs as well as of attachment to the spirit.

ABRAHAM HESCHEL[1]

ON PRAYER
Each breath attended to,
every step taken with true intention,
every rambling thought let go of,
every slight pause before acting
hollows out a broad place in the
centre of one's being,
a deepened uncramped place where
apathy and cynicism are replaced
with the flow of compassion.
This essentially is the miracle of prayer.

DAY ONE

Desire

May he grant you your heart's desire,
and fulfill all your plans.

PSALM 20:4

Whom have I in heaven but you? And there is
nothing on earth that I desire other than you.
My flesh and my heart fail, but God is the strength
of my heart and my portion forever.

PSALM 73:25

OUR DESIRES WILL greatly influence the direction of our journey. Every seeking is guided beforehand by what is sought.

In Mark 10, Jesus asks a blind man, "What do you want me to do for you?" At first the question may seem straightforward. In a way it is. The difficulty may come when we try to answer it. We need to dig down into our strata of longings, through the frivolous surface desires and deeper to those we feel strongly about, until we approach the core. There we find the singular desire that lies at the centre of our being. Underneath every other human longing is the longing for love. "As a deer longs for the flowing stream, so my soul longs for you, O God" (Psalm 42).

We spend much of our time and energy trying to satisfy our desires. Many desires are responsible or virtuous. We desire the best for our children, health for ourselves and our loved ones, maybe even peace on earth. Yet even the most virtuous of our myriad desires will not lead us to waters that will satisfy our deepest thirst, unless we pause to touch our greatest desire, the longing for God.

Recently, the worship committee of our church met to plan a strategy for the coming year. During a playful and contemplative interlude I asked, "What do you really want from the worship experience?" After some silence one person spoke, "I want to know I have experienced God." Then another, "I want to be able to give all my worries and anxieties to God." Another said, "I want to know I am truly connected to my church family." The last person to share said, "I want sermons I can understand." All these desires represent authentic longings.

Surely, if we invest time and energy in something there must be results! Many understand faith in this pragmatic way. We attend church, pray, and worship so that we will experience an enhanced self-image, mend a relationship, or have answers for difficult questions. This view of spirituality is deeply ingrained in our result-oriented culture. Still, the yearnings of our church committee members skirted around the deep and central longing for God. I am not encouraging you to censure your desires, for they may be good and authentic. Instead, I encourage you to investigate your desires to find your inmost longing.

Feel the weight of these two questions: What do I really want? What's in it for me? The answers to the two questions may determine how deeply into Sabbath we go. Love's invitation is to look beyond our longings for happiness, peace, prosperity, power, success, health, recovery, satisfaction, and fulfillment. This is not an easy endeavour. Mentally sifting through our many desires to identify our one true desire requires perseverance and grace. We fill our lives with things that excite us for a moment, but when the excitement wears off we search for something new. We are stuffed but insatiable at the same time.

The unfolding of our deepest desire is a life-long process. At first we may notice only brief glimpses of it. It may take many Sabbath moments, over years, to discern our true desire. "Six days a week we wrestle with the world, wringing profit from the earth; on the Sabbath we especially care for the seed of eternity planted in the soul."[2] Sabbath time is the time between all our doing, all our plans and desires, when we catch a glimpse of love itself.

This week you are invited to explore your deepest desire. Initially, it may feel strange and unfamiliar. However, when you stop to look and listen to your heart and what is most authentic, you may find that realizing your desire for love is like a reunion with a long-lost friend.

FOR REFLECTION

Loving God, please grant me the grace to discover and hold my deepest desire before you.

If you had a computer program that could create a virtual reality what would it be like? As you focus on the desires that surface, see if there is one that goes a little deeper. Follow these different levels of desire to see where they lead.

INTENTION ***Today I ask, "What do I want?" As my many desires surface, I pause to see whether there is a deeper one underneath all the others.***

BREATH PRAYER

BREATHING IN *I am my beloved's,*

BREATHING OUT *and his desire is for me*

SONG OF SOLOMON 7:10

DAY TWO

Stopping

One's life does not consist in the abundance of possessions. Then he [Jesus] told them a parable: The land of a rich man produced abundantly. And he thought to himself, "What should I do, for I have no place to store my crops?" Then he said, "I will do this: I will pull down my barns and build larger ones, and there I will store all my grain and my goods. And I will say to my soul, 'Soul, you have ample goods laid up for many years; relax, eat, drink, be merry.'" But God said to him, "You fool! This very night your life is being demanded of you. And the things you have prepared, whose will they be?" So it is with those who store up treasures for themselves but are not rich toward God.

LUKE 12:15–21

WHAT DO YOU want to be when you grow up? This is a question we ask children even before they have a concept of the day-after-tomorrow. Early in our lives we are taught that we are what we do. Add to this the prevailing myth that time is money, money is power, and power makes the world go round, and we have a culture whose people worship work. Our cheque books and investments (vestment, a religious garment) represent our security (Latin *securus*, free from care). Sam Keen describes the idolatrous dilemma that has unfolded in our culture thus:

> In the secular theology of economic man [*sic*] work has replaced God as the source from whom all blessings flow. The escalating gross national product, or at least the rising Dow Jones index, is the outward and visible sign that we are progressing toward the Kingdom of God; full employment is grace, unemployment is sin. The industrious, especially entrepreneurs with capital, are God's chosen people, but the laborers are sanctified because they participate in the productive economy.[3]

Sabbath is a subversive act. When we pause for breath we are rebelling against the idolatry of productivity. Sabbath involves a conscious work stoppage that lets us discover that our real identity is not in what we do or what we produce, but in who we are. Sabbath helps us pause and notice what is really here.

This poem is a reflection on the story of a woman accused of adultery found in John 8.

PAUSE

when Jesus paused –
oh the sweet sound
of the word pause –

when he stooped to
the ground and
wrote in the dust

and the good
Yahweh-loving folks who
wanted to teach him truth

dropped their stones
one by one
beginning with the oldest

and with their stones
all the ammunition
their hearts could hold

judgement, reactivity,
orthodoxy, certainty,
self-righteousness

I wonder if he was
making an opening in the
dusty ground of being

that tapped into
the ever-flowing
stream of life

just below the
thin surface of
all our reactivity

so what bubbled
up from beneath
were the healing waters

in which he
baptized the woman
and Pharisees alike

in total acceptance and
essential blessing. . .
all in the Sabbath pause

STOPPING

For most of us it's not easy. No matter how fast we go, no matter how many sacrifices we make to quicken our pace, there never seems to be enough time. Amazing innovations were going to free great stretches of our days for what counts: friends, family, and fun, but the opposite has happened. We've witnessed the proliferation of dazzling, timesaving innovations: jet travel, personal computers, fax machines, cellphones, microwaves, fast-food restaurants, and the ultimate timesaver, the Internet. Yet the pace of our lives has spiralled upward to the point that our grandparents scratch their heads in disbelief, and we are left breathless.

The fool in Jesus' parable sold out to the idol of productivity. He could not bear the concept of Sabbath, let alone attempt to practice it! Even when his barns were full he could not pause in gratitude, but was anxious to keep busy and move on to the next project. That story, along with the Old Testament teachings of Sabbath, demonstrates that a person who does not take the time to pause for breath, thus imitating the Creator in rest, is a person headed for self-destruction. If we are too busy to stop for breath, we are too busy. All exhaling and no inhaling – no wonder we're breathless!

Sabbath is about stopping. The subversive act of coming to a stop can help move us from a less-than-conscious, results-driven place to a conscious, free, and trusting place. It's time to stop before we forget who we are.

And how do we begin to apply life's brakes when the world around us is stomping on the gas pedal? Three words guide us; prayerfully, gently, and patiently. Just for a moment, try something radical. Put a stop to all the input in your life. Try this for five minutes a day for a week. Once we assure ourselves that the world will not fly off its tracks when we stop racing, we'll find it isn't that arduous, and we'll want more.

FOR REFLECTION

Consider this passage from Mark 4:35–41.

> On that day, when evening had come, he [Jesus] said to them, "Let us go across to the other side." And leaving the crowd behind, they took him with them in the boat, just as he was. Other boats were with him. A great windstorm arose, and the waves beat into the boat, so that the boat was already being swamped. But he was in the stern, asleep on the cushion; and they woke him up and said to him, "Teacher, do you not care that we are perishing?" He woke up and rebuked the wind, and

said to the sea, "Peace! Be still!" Then the wind ceased, and there was a dead calm. He said to them, "Why are you afraid? Have you still no faith?" And they were filled with great awe and said to one another, "Who then is this, that even the wind and the sea obey him?"

Read this passage through at a normal pace. Pause for a moment and read it again, very slowly, perhaps out loud. Pause for a longer time and notice what image or phrase from the text draws you to it.

Sit with this image or phrase for a few more minutes, repeating it slowly a few times.

What might God be saying to you?

What is your response?

INTENTION **Today I stop and acknowledge God's presence in me.**

BREATH PRAYER

BREATHING IN **Be still and know**

BREATHING OUT **that I am God**

PSALM 46:10

DAY THREE

Looking

God saw that it was good.

GENESIS 1:10

Again Jesus spoke to them saying, "I am the light of the world. Whoever follows me will never walk in darkness but will have the light of life."

JOHN 8:12

WHEN WE ARE driving in a car the world whirls by quickly and we notice very little. When we walk the same route, we are amazed at all the delightful details. However, when we stop on the path, we really see what's there.

Sabbath is stopping to contemplate. Sabbath is taking a long, loving look at the truth. Sabbath practice helps us to see the world from the perspective of paying attention, which I believe is prayer. Prayer is a compassionate look at what is most real in ourselves and in the world around us. Opening our souls to see how God's light shines on us is Sabbath prayer.

Given the hectic pace of our lives, we merely skim the surface of the extravagant beauty that abundantly embraces us. We barely touch experiences that can be magically transformative, and then we hurry on to do something else. Even if we think we are relaxing, we are usually rushing from one experience to another. Sabbath allows wonderful opportunities to consider the lilies, the birds of the air, your own heartbeat, a child's laughter, or whatever beautiful thing there is before you. Those who embrace Sabbath practice take the time to notice life.

Oh, by the way, the Gospels suggest these activities go a long way to reducing worry and stress!

FOR REFLECTION

Consider Annie Dillard's description of her world.

> About five years ago I saw a mockingbird make a straight descent from the roof gutter of a four-story building. It was an act as careless and spontaneous as the curl of a stem or the kindling of a star. The mockingbird took a single step into the air and, dropped. His wings were still folded against his sides as though he were swinging from a limb and not falling, accelerating thirty-two feet per second, through empty air. Just a breath before he would have been dashed to the ground, he unfurled his wings with exact, deliberate care, revealing the broad bars of white, spread his elegant, white-banded tail, and so floated onto the grass. I had just rounded a corner when his insouciant step caught my eye; there was no one else in sight. The fact of his free fall was like the old philosophical conundrum about the tree that falls in the forest. The answer must be, I think that beauty and grace are performed whether or not we will or sense them. The least we can do is try to be there.[4]

A different way of viewing the world is epitomized in the now-famous whole-earth picture of our planet from the NASA files. It is an astounding photograph of the earth as a blue and white marble floating in black, empty space, lonely and vulnerable. Although for many it has become the icon of the environmental movement, truly it is a picture that is without detail; clean and sterile. The whole-earth view simplifies and objectifies the earth. It is the spectator's view, "a blue and white Christmas ornament," as one astronaut described it.[5]

This spectator's view of earth is also considered by some to be a God's-eye view, as if God is distant, removed, unconcerned about the intricacies and individuals of the earth's inhabitants. Many people relate to the earth this way too – from a distance and disconnected – a perspective that might just as well be from three thousand miles away.

Do we look at other people this way too? Do we bother to look at people closely, as individuals with histories, families, and dreams? Do we class groups of people all together – those blacks or those whites? Are we convinced that our reality is the only true reality? Do we respect the differences in others? Disconnection can literally suffocate our whole being. Sabbath is time to notice what is really there.

Become reacquainted with yourself. Go to a museum. Plant a tree. Sit on a bench and watch people. Spend time with a caterpillar. Walk in the woods. Bake a loaf of bread from scratch. Consider the lilies and allow wonder to be reborn in you.

INTENTION **Today I pause for a long, loving look at the beauty in and around me.**

BREATH PRAYER

BREATHING IN *Open my eyes that I may see*

BREATHING OUT *glimpses of truth thou hast for me*

DAY FOUR

Listening

And when you turn to the right or when you turn to the left, your ears shall hear a word behind you, saying, "This is the way; walk in it."

ISAIAH 30:21

I HOPE YOU have decided to try stopping for a while. How's it going? Have you noticed how distractions rise so easily in the Sabbath pause? Consider these two definitions of "to distract":

1. To cause to turn away from the original focus or interest; divert;
2. To pull in conflicting emotional directions; unsettle.[6]

When we stop, we begin to touch a deep desire that is full of life and light. As we are increasingly drawn to times of prayer, to times spent in the light of grace, we may be intolerant of the distractions that bother us when we create our Sabbath space. Shopping lists, noises, memories, daydreams, aches and pains, fantasies, feelings, and fears all vie for our attention. It may seem that the harder we try to focus, the sharper these distractions appear. So, do we give in and yield to their siren calls?

During one Sabbath moment, I joyfully discovered that it was better to join these distractions than fight them! When I enter into a Sabbath place and the residuals of the day begin to float like jetsam across the screen of my mind, I don't forcefully ignore or chase them away. I actually just let myself become more aware of them. Yet, in this holy place of Sabbath rest, I don't feel compelled to respond to their demands. I just acknowledge them. Now they become easier to set aside for later. Ponder these words of John Donne.

> I throw myself down in my chamber, and I call in, and invite
> God, and his angels thither, and when they are there, I neglect
> God and his angels for the noise of a fly, for the rattle of a coach,
> for the whining of a door.[7]

We are so attached to the things in and around us that we can't hear or notice God's presence! Actually, it's not "the noise of the fly, or the rattle of the coach, or the whining of a door" that is the root of our attachment and unsettledness. It's that we are attached to familiar, and therefore secure, things. It takes practice to learn to let these things be present without turning away from our prayer.

The Sabbath pause helps nurture a growing awareness of God's presence. Ultimately, Sabbath can lead us to experience pure prayer where the soul is in a state of union with God and there is peace. However, moments like this may be rare. Be gentle with yourself as your prayer life unfolds. Discover what works best for you. Don't judge your experience against your notion of ideal prayer. Relax and allow the invitation of Sabbath practice to lead you as you listen for God. Look for God in any experience of life. Stop. Look. Listen. God is present and active in all life.

FOR REFLECTION

In order to hear what you may have been missing, give attention today to the quiet. Try rising early before dawn to listen to the sounds of the approaching day. What does God's "voice" sound like for you?

Find music that reminds you of holiness. Try music of the Taizé community, or Gregorian chant. What song do you carry in your heart today?

INTENTION **Today when I pray I gently listen for God in all the noise in my life.**

BREATH PRAYER

BREATHING IN *In this pause*

BREATHING OUT *I hear God's whisper*

DAY FIVE

Intentions

*Your heavenly Father knows that you need
these things. But strive first for the kingdom of God
and its righteousness and all these things will be
given to you as well.*

MATTHEW 6:32, 33

*Many people have a wrong idea of what constitutes
true happiness. It is not attained through self-
gratification but through fidelity to a worthy cause.*

HELEN KELLER[8]

WE BEGAN THIS week by focusing on our desires. Each day
we have been invited to stop, look at, and listen to our desires.
The invitation has been to notice the many desires that lie near the
surface of our lives and then gently allow our deepest desire, our most
powerful longing, to surface. We long for Love. And when we learn
that we desire God more than anything, we may also discover that God
longs for us too.

Once we become more familiar with our deepest desire for Love, we are ready to respond to Love's invitation. Intention is what focuses our response to the longing. "Desire is wanting something, longing for some satisfaction. Intention is claiming the wanting, consciously owning it, choosing to seek satisfaction."[9]

When I was a teenager my father gave me a calendar from his plumbing and heating business. Each month had a saying, as well as a picture of a faucet or a heating element. One of the sayings is indelibly printed in my memory: "Dream deep for each dream precedes the goal." I see this as an invitation to set aside the limiting confines of talents or abilities, the restraints of our history, the inhibitions of our personalities and to dream, dream deep, so that our dreams guide our actions.

Intention literally means stretching. When we allow a desire to surface, our will is stretched, reaching out to what we deeply long for. Intention is subtly different from sheer determination. It is not a grasping, a forceful, manipulative taking of what we desire. God's love is freely given. Our intention toward this gift involves more of an open-handed receiving than a grasping fist. It is an open stretching toward God, who is stretching toward us.

This is the collaborative nature of Sabbath. We and God meet when we enter Sabbath. This requires two things: awakening to God's loving presence, and divine grace. "Awakening is needed for appreciation; we cannot be intentional when we are asleep. Grace is needed for empowerment: for making intention possible in the first place, and for bringing it to fruition."[10]

Intention is everything; it puts the flesh of action on our bare-boned desires. Desire only wants to respond to Love's invitation. Intention moves us toward Love. In our Sabbath time, awakening and grace become holy ground. Everything is transformed.

FOR REFLECTION

Consider Paul's advice: "Let the same mind be in you that was in Christ Jesus, who, though he was in the form of God, did not regard equality with God to be in the grasping but in the emptying" (Philippians 2:3, my translation).

Intentions are like blueprints. They allow us to give shape and content to our desires. Intentions can also serve as trail markers along our Sabbath journey so we follow God's path for us. When we trust that our deepest desire touches God's desire for us, we can more clearly discern God's will for our journey. Is there a question you need to discern or a direction in which you need leading? Ask, "What do I really want?" See what answer surfaces.

> *Work as if the money doesn't matter.*
> *Love as if you have never been hurt.*
> *Dance as if no one is watching.*
> *Follow your heart's desire as if you had wings.*
> SATCHEL PAIGE[11]

INTENTION **Today my deepest dreams move me to some action.**

BREATH PRAYER

BREATHING IN **In this silence I wait**

BREATHING OUT **ready to receive God's gifts**

Review

IN OUR CHURCH we use a bell at the beginning of the worship service to usher us into a time and space that is separate from other times in our lives. Sabbath time is a time separate from the time we spend working, producing, achieving, or even playing. It is not that we escape these things in our Sabbath practice; we carry them with us. But there is a subtle separateness or holiness about Sabbath that is qualitatively different from the rest of our time. When moved by our deep desire for Love we stop, look, and listen. We learn that Sabbath time is the best of times and that it subtly but truly transforms all the rest of our time. "Then Sabbath is not for the sake of the weekdays; the weekdays are for the sake of Sabbath. It is not an interlude but the climax of living."[12]

Our lives are often muddled, mixed-up, dulled. The separateness of Sabbath time helps us see more clearly how we are in relationship with God and others.

One of the most beautiful descriptions of the nature of intimate human relationship is found in the book by Rilke, *On Love and Other Difficulties*. As you read this, consider how our human relationship mirrors our relationship with God.

> It is a question in marriage, to my feeling, not of creating a quick community of spirit by tearing down and destroying all boundaries, but rather a good marriage is that in which each appoints the other guardian of his solitude, and shows him this confidence, the greatest in his power to bestow. A togetherness

between two people is an impossibility, and where it seems, nevertheless, to exist, it is a narrowing, a reciprocal agreement which robs either one party or both of his fullest freedom and development. But, once the realization is accepted that even between the closest human beings infinite distances continue to exist, a wonderful living side by side can grow up, if they succeed in loving the distance between them which makes it possible for each to see the other whole and against a wide sky. Therefore this too must be the standard for rejection or choice: Whether one is willing to stand guard over the solitude of a person and whether one is inclined to set this same person at the gate of one's own solitude, of which he learns only through that which steps, festively clothed, out of the great darkness.[13]

FOR REFLECTION

Did you take (or receive) the time to stop, look, and listen this week?

What metaphors can you use to describe Sabbath time? This week my Sabbath time

felt like . . .

seemed like . . .

tasted like . . .

appeared like . . .

lingered like . . .

sounded like . . .

INTENTION **Today I give thanks for the gift of increasing clarity.**

BREATH PRAYER

BREATHING IN *I can be filled*

BREATHING OUT *only when I am empty*

DAY SEVEN

Sabbath Group

OPENING PRAYER (TOGETHER)

God, our lives can be so busy. We learned as children to stop, look, and listen before we cross a busy street. You have invited us to cross over into a Sabbath place of rest and trust. This is the one journey that really matters. It is the journey into the place of stillness that is deep within us. We know that to reach that place is to be at home with you, and to fail to reach it is to remain stuck in our restlessness. Precious God, take our hands. Like a loving parent, hold us in your awesome grip as we cross this dangerous intersection.

Leader: This week we have been reminded of how subversive and countercultural Sabbath practice is. This is a high calling, a sacred journey. Much is at stake. Our rest and our peace, and much more, depend on the choices we make at the busy intersections of life. Today we are reminded that we are not alone on this journey but share in community. And God is with us.

BREATH PRAYER (TOGETHER)

BREATHING IN *My soul is at rest*

BREATHING OUT *in God alone*

After two or three minutes of silence, the group joins in the song "Precious Lord, Take My Hand."[14]

SHARING TIME

How have you touched your deeper desires this week?

Try an exercise in spiritual archeology. Divide into groups of two and share your desires. What do you want? Ask each other the question three to five times. See what you uncover.

Use the *lectio divina* practice (see page 75) with the passage from Luke 12 below.

> Then Jesus said to his disciples: "Therefore I tell you, do not worry about your life, what you will eat; or about your body, what you will wear. Life is more than food, and the body more than clothes. Consider the ravens: They do not sow or reap, they have no storeroom or barn; yet God feeds them. And how much more valuable you are than birds! Who of you by worrying can add a single hour to his life? Since you cannot do this very little thing, why do you worry about the rest? Consider how the lilies grow. They do not labor or spin. Yet I tell you, not even Solomon in all his splendor was dressed like one of these. If that is how God clothes the grass of the field, which is here today, and tomorrow is thrown into the fire, how much more will he clothe you, O you of little faith! And do not set your heart on what you will eat or drink; do not worry about it. For the pagan world runs after all such things, and your Father knows that you need them. But seek his kingdom, and these things will be given to you as well. Do not be afraid, little flock, for your Father has been pleased to give you the kingdom. Sell your possessions and give to the poor.

Provide purses for yourselves that will not wear out, a treasure in heaven that will not be exhausted, where no thief comes near and no moth destroys. For where your treasure is, there your heart will be also."

After the *lectio* exercise, sing verse two of "Precious Lord, Take My Hand."[15]

BLESSING (TOGETHER)
The Lord is near. Let us not worry about anything but in everything by prayer and supplication with thanksgiving let our requests be made known to God. And the peace of God, which surpasses all understanding, will guard our hearts and our minds in Christ Jesus. Amen. (Philippians 4:5–7)

Sabbath Is Simple

*Now God saw all that he had made and here: it
was exceedingly good! There was setting, there was
dawning: the sixth day.*

GENESIS 1:31

SIMPLE PRAISE

*on this morning's walk in the rain
i heard a symphony of voices*

*the droplet on the pine needle
invited me to distill my longings*

*the turtle on the path
reminded me to slow down*

*the persistently gentle Cedar Creek
assured me that life always finds the way*

the autumn leaves beneath the scrub oak
called me to let go too

the long narrow lonely path
reminded me that i will not get lost

and the rain. . . the rain
a baptism from above
a soft and tender whisper
with every drop that fell
offering a simple one word
praise that echoed back
from the deepest well within me

yes, yes, yes, yes, yes,
a million times yes

let the earth rejoice
and all that is within it
praise the lord

DAY ONE

Uncluttered

...for one's life does not consist in the abundance of possessions.

LUKE 12:15

I'M OVERWHELMED BY clutter and want help to restore control over my space, time, and life." This is the desperate concern of a woman I know. She attends weekly meetings of a support group called Clutterers Anonymous. Much of her time is spent struggling to "declutter" her life.

The clutter disorder plagues many people. "It's very widespread," says Aimee McHale, Tenant Coordinator for Mission Housing Development Corporation in San Francisco, "and we are eager to understand it as well as to assist our residents in applying the strategies for addressing it."[1]

McHale explains that many individuals gather more belongings than their rooms can accommodate. Often difficulties arise when a small room is packed with belongings or debris and the resident can no longer access an exit in case of fire. In some cases, individuals can no longer use their bathtub, bed, or table.

People suffering from this disorder, who are known in the vernacular as "pack rats," feel compelled to gather items out of an overwhelming fear of being without a needed item. Some sufferers cannot throw out their daily incoming mail or even food wrappings. Since they fear they'll throw out something important, they find themselves fearful of throwing out anything at all. The result is a storeroom, often packed to the ceiling. "It's ruining my life," said one man, a sufferer of this syndrome. "I wish I knew how to heal myself."

The best clinical treatment for obsessive-compulsive hoarding is cognitive-behavioural therapy. The success rate of this technique to treat obsessive compulsive disorder (OCD) is high, especially when combined with anti-depressant medication. It requires the sufferer to face the feared situation in small increments, and to tolerate that exposure. For a hoarder, the exposures would be the feared situation of not collecting new material, and the feared situation of throwing something out.

Like many people, you may feel as if your life and your space are too full of stuff. We too often spend money we don't have to buy things we don't need to impress people we don't even like. The stuff adds up. If our living space is cluttered with all kinds of things, it can (and will) create emotional, physical, and spiritual imbalances.

Clutter can happen in our inner lives too. If our inner lives are cluttered with anger, depression, worry, or anxiety, the clutter disease can cause spiritual sluggishness or even paralysis. As we create Sabbath time and space in our lives we will find that our body, mind, and spirit will become more harmonious. I entered one such Sabbath moment recently very early in the morning. As I sat quietly I considered some of the clutter, inner and outer, that invades my life. As I thought about getting rid of some of this clutter I felt afraid. What was I afraid of?

ONE SIMPLE SABBATH MORNING

In the stillness of this Sabbath morning
I became aware
of that strange mixture
of will and spirit,
choice and grace.

Life blood and water
mingled into one and
flowed out from my centre
like a plug had been pulled
or a dam broken,
leaving behind emptiness.

What if I let go
of the things that "comfort" me?
Would God be my comfort?
What if I let go
of my sure and certain constructs
that range from neuroses to faith?
What if I let go
of my insatiable need to control
people, things, time?
What if, and how?

As I sat in the quiet…
the sound of a garbage truck intruded
Stop – Start
Clutch – Shift
Hydraulic fluids straining
to compress the load.

Once burgeoning cans
now lie empty on the sidewalk
waiting to store more refuse
for next week's pick-up.

What if the garbage was left
to pile up, rot, decay
in the house?

There will always be the need
to be emptied
for there is much waste.
Even the recyclables have to
go out to be processed.

So I must be emptied
even of that which is good
and useful
before I am given the
fresh and new.

This happened one simple
Sabbath morning.

FOR REFLECTION

Better is a handful with quietness than both hands
full with travail and striving after the wind.

ECCLESIASTES 4:6

What would you grab if your house was on fire? Offer a prayer of gratitude for these things you cherish.

To discover simplicity in your life, imagine sifting through all that is trivial and not essential until you discover what lies close to your passion, like finding a diamond in the sand. Choose an object you cherish. Hold it in your hand. Feel its weight in your hand and its tug on your heart.

What is your prayer space like? Are there objects in it that are not beautiful or meaningful? Why not start here to clean some clutter from your life?

INTENTION **Today I notice what gives me joy and what weighs me down.**

BREATH PRAYER

BREATHING IN **You satisfy**

BREATHING OUT **the hungry heart**

DAY TWO

Yielding

To be at the leading edge of consumption, affluence and instant gratification is to be at the dying edge. To ignore the dignity of work and the elegance of simplicity, and essential responsibility of serving each other is to be at the dying edge. Justice Oliver Wendell Holmes is reported to have said about simplicity, "I would not give a fig for the simplicity this side of complexity, but I would give my life for the simplicity on the other side of complexity." To be at the livening edge is to search out the simplicity on the other side of complexity.

MAX DE PREE[2]

DON'T FIGHT THE current! Swim down shore!" These words saved my brother's life. Ron was swimming in the ocean off the Virginia coastline when he got caught in a dangerous riptide. The strong current was pulling him out to sea. He fought in vain to swim against it toward the shore a short distance away. The harder he tried, the more exhausted he became. He began to panic, as did his wife who stood on the shore. A nearby fisherman, who knew about riptides, came to the rescue by shouting the life-saving directions. Not to swim directly for the nearby shore went against his every instinct because safety was only a few yards away. But after yielding to the current's pull, he swam sideways out of the rip and then safely to the beach.

Sabbath time is an opportunity to redirect our lives. We think we know what will save us. If only we could reach the shore. If only we could have more success, more time, more stuff. If only we were married to a different person, had a better job, or more education. We spend most of our economic and psychological resources grasping for life preservers, yet somehow we never seem to be able to reach the shore. How close are we to going under?

Should Ron have felt guilty for trying to swim straight to the shore? Of course not. Every fibre of his being told him that this was the simple course to take. Yet if he had persisted he would have drowned. Should we feel guilty about our fantasies of a simpler life on the shores of "if only"? Fantasies can come from our shadow side, but even so they teach us something about our human sensibilities. Beneath our discontent is our deep longing for God.

Saint Bernard wrote that our essential human nature is rooted in our creation in the image of God. "God is love and there is nothing in all created things which is able to fill the creature who has been made in God's image except the love which is God. For God alone is greater than the human image."[3]

Sabbath teaches us the discipline of "learning how to have our fantasies and stand aside from them simultaneously." This apparently contradictory stance is intrinsic in all subsequent movements of the spiritual life."[4]

What are your fantasies? What do you dream or daydream about? Chances are they have something to do with five common human priorities:

1. The need to be invulnerable;
2. The desire to be uninhibited;
3. The yearning for validation;
4. The longing for intimacy;
5. The wish to be whole.[5]

FOR REFLECTION

In the following passage notice how the followers of Jesus yielded to his command and presence.

After these things Jesus showed himself again to the disciples by the Sea of Tiberias; and he showed himself in this way. Gathered there together were Simon Peter, Thomas called the Twin, Nathaniel of Cana in Galilee, the sons of Zebedee, and two others of his disciples. Simon Peter said to them, "I am going fishing." They said to him, "We will go with you." They went out and got into the boat, but that night they caught nothing.

Just after daybreak, Jesus stood on the beach; but the disciples did not know that it was Jesus. Jesus said to them "Children, you have no fish, have you?" They answered him, "No." He said to them, "Cast the net to the right side of the boat, and you will find some." So they cast it, and now they were not able to haul it in because there were so many fish. That disciple whom Jesus loved said to Peter, "It is the Lord!" When Simon

Peter heard that it was the Lord, he put on some clothes, for he was naked, and jumped into the sea. But the other disciples came in the boat, dragging the net full of fish, for they were not far from the land, only about a hundred yards off.

When they had gone ashore, they saw a charcoal fire there, with fish on it, and bread. Jesus said to them, "Bring some of the fish that you have just caught." So Simon Peter went aboard and hauled the net ashore, full of large fish, a hundred fifty-three of them; and though there were so many, the net was not torn. Jesus said to them, "Come and have breakfast." Now none of the disciples dared to ask him, "Who are you?" because they knew it was the Lord. Jesus came and took the bread and gave it to them, and did the same with the fish. This was now the third time that Jesus appeared to the disciples after he was raised from the dead.

JOHN 21:1–14

INTENTION **Today I relax and trust the current of the Spirit to take me where it will.**

Breath Prayer

BREATHING IN *With each breath*

BREATHING OUT *I let go*

DAY THREE

Trust

*Now the two of them, the human and his wife, were
nude, yet they were not ashamed.*

GENESIS 2:25[6]

*The eyes of the two of them were opened and then
they knew that they were nude. They sewed fig leaves
together and made themselves loincloths. Now they
heard the sound of YHWH, God, (who was) walking
about in the garden at the breezy-time of the day.
And the human and his wife hid themselves from the
face of YHWH, God amid the trees of the garden.
YHMH, God, called to the human and said to him,
"Where are you?"*

GENESIS 3:7–9[7]

I HAVE LEARNED FROM my children that we are born with the capability to trust. It is distrust that we must learn. Life's lessons begin very early and are thorough. Lesson one in skepticism begins in early infancy as the baby experiences the disappointment when mother's breast is not always there on demand. So begins a steady stream of life's lessons, which teach us that life is not always the way it's supposed to be, or at least the way we think it's supposed to be. We learn to cope with diminishing confidence in and increasing suspicion of not only of others, but "the system," ourselves, and God as well. *That's life* and similar platitudes fail to give real comfort.

The Hebrew language has a beautiful word, *shalom*, to describe the way things are supposed to be. Sometimes shalom is translated "peace." Actually it means far more. It means the webbing together of all of creation in a universal flourishing of wholeness and delight in a relationship of rightness in God. This is what the Creator intended. Sin is vandalism of shalom. Sin "violates shalom because it breaks the peace, because it interferes with the way things are supposed to be."[8]

The story of Adam and Eve is a story of original trust, or shalom, and how it was ravaged by sin. The rest of the story is about the rebuilding of trust. Listen to the words of God as recorded in Revelation 21.

> And the one who was seated on the throne said, "See, I am making all things new." Also he said, "Write this, for these words are trustworthy and true." Then he said to me, "It is done! I Am the Alpha and the Omega, the beginning and the end. To the thirsty I will give water as a gift from the spring of the water of life."

I have often thought that my relationship with God vacillates between intimacy and resistance. Intimacy is built on trust. Trust is needed to allow "in-to-me-see." Resistance is built on mistrust. Because of disappointment, betrayal, or fear, which are all a part of broken shalom, I sometimes choose not to let anyone in, especially God. With the doors of my heart closed, all the hatches battened down, my soul is diminished.

My capacity to be intimate with God, or for that matter with anyone, is a gift that is nourished in Sabbath moments. Those are the moments where I become like a child, if only for a moment, basking in the joy of original trust.

God tells us straightforwardly through Jesus, "Unless you change and become like a child, you will never enter the Kingdom of Heaven" (Matthew 18:3). That seems to speak of something that is possible for us now. It refers to something that is already a present reality for us, albeit layered with the lessons of mistrust. Often Jesus says, "The reign of heaven is at hand." He does not say, "The reign of heaven is my promise for the future." Instead he tells us that this reign is what is here now. God's presence is among us. We will recognize that Presence when we again become as little children, when we allow the layers of defences and false images to be stripped away and we become who we really are.

FOR REFLECTION

> *Surely God is my salvation;*
> *I will trust, and will not be afraid,*
> *for the Lord God is my strength and my might;*
> *he has become my salvation.*

ISAIAH 12:2

> *In returning and rest you shall be saved;*
> *in quietness and in trust shall be your strength.*

ISAIAH 30:16

INTENTION **Today I remember when I trusted as a child before betrayal. I am aware of that same child living within me and wanting to trust again.**

BREATH PRAYER

BREATHING IN *I will trust*

BREATHING OUT *and not be afraid*

DAY FOUR

Gift

God loves a cheerful giver. And God is able to provide you with every blessing in abundance, so that by always having enough of everything, you may share abundantly in every good work. As it is written, "He scatters abroad, he gives to the poor; his righteousness endures forever." He who supplies seed to the sower and bread for food will supply and multiply your seed for sowing and increase the harvest of your righteousness. You will be enriched in every way for your great generosity, which will produce thanksgiving to God through us; for the rendering of this ministry not only supplies the needs of the saints but also overflows with many thanksgivings to God. Through the testing of this ministry you glorify God by your obedience to the confession of the gospel of Christ and by the generosity of your sharing with them and with all others, while they long for you and pray for you because of the surpassing grace of God that he has given you. Thanks be to God for his indescribable gift!

2 CORINTHIANS 9:7B–15

CHRISTMAS MORNING AT our house is a paradox of mayhem and peace. The children's wide-eyed wonder, the smells of the tree and freshly brewed coffee, and the energy of anticipation all create a wonderful Sabbath-like celebration. What if, after all the preparations were made, all the decorations hung, all the gifts wrapped, we just sat and stared at them? "Nice wrapping. Let's eat."

How many gifts lie unopened in our lives?

Sabbath is an opportunity to taste of God's generosity. It is a gift that keeps on giving. It's a beautifully wrapped package that only gets more beautiful as we unwrap it. Most of us don't feel deserving of gifts, and find it easier to give than to receive. Our pride and our stubborn individualism make it hard to imagine a God who would lavish indescribable gifts on us. We feel we must earn our gifts. Sabbath is an opportunity to receive and luxuriate in the gifts of God.

Recently I had a meeting with a friend who is a top executive at Goldman Sachs. We meet in her office in Jersey City, New Jersey, which had a beautiful view of the New York skyline. While waiting in the lobby outside her office I was captivated by what I saw on the wall.

THE GIFT OF THE QUILT
on the 34th floor of the
Goldman Sachs world headquarters
in the department of "human capital"
lives a quilt displayed behind glass

its fine stitches
and soft colors
are undiminished
by its long 100-year life

nor is the beauty
warmth and comfort
it offers without effect
in the halls of acquisition

where if one didn't know better
one would think that it was
an overpaid decorator's attempt
to hide a cold interior

no, it is the artist's beauty
subversively intruding on the
economist's space reaching out
to passersby with a gift

the spirit of the Amish
women whose nimble
fingers and sharp eyes
gave the gift is still there giving

so that those who live with
the quilt along with the balance
sheets and financial projections
will remember the simple truth

always known that in everything there
is a soul that longs for beauty
that is more precious than
silver and brighter than gold.

The truth of the Sabbath is this: If we stop long enough, with open hands, God fills us with good things. Sabbath makes space for God's gifts. When we become emptier, whether inwardly or outwardly, we can become a proper home for God. "Bless the Lord, O my soul...who satisfies you with good as long as you live" (Psalm 103).

FOR REFLECTION

You have made us masters of your world, to tend it, to serve it, to enjoy it. For six days we measure and we build, we count and carry the real and imagined burdens of our task, the success we earn and the price we pay. On this, the Sabbath day, give us time.[9]

Fill for yourselves water from the living spring
of the Lord,
because it has been opened for you.
And come all you thirsty and take a drink, and rest
beside the spring of the Lord because it is pleasing
and sparkling, and perpetually pleases the self.
For more refreshing is its water than honey,
and the honeycomb of bees is not to be compared with it;
Because it flowed from the lips of the Lord, and it was
named from the heart of the Lord.
And it came boundless and invisible,
and until it was set in the middle they knew it not.
Blessed are they who have drunk from it, and
have rested by it.
Hallelujah!

ODES OF SOLOMON 30:–7[10]

INTENTION **Today I am satisfied with God's abundant gifts.**

BREATH PRAYER

BREATHING IN *I now receive*

BREATHING OUT *everything I need*

DAY FIVE

Rest

Thus says the Lord: Stand at the crossroads, and look, and ask for the ancient paths, where the good way lies; and walk in it, and find rest for your souls.

JEREMIAH 6:16

Come to me all who are carrying heavy burdens, and I will give you rest. Take my yoke upon you, and learn from me; for I am gentle and humble in heart, and you will find rest for your souls. For my yoke is easy, and my burden is light.

MATTHEW 11:28

A FRIEND OF MINE is an executive in a rapidly growing "start-up" company. He works a lot. He makes a great deal of money. He is very stressed. I have been encouraging him to allow Sabbath time to enter his life. He resists, saying, "I know that if I take the time to rest someone else will be working, maybe getting ahead of me." I am afraid he is addicted to work.

Workaholism has been called the cleanest of all addictions. It is socially acceptable and even encouraged because it is productive. But at what cost? Families suffer, health declines, and spiritual bankruptcy, the final symptom of workaholism, usually heralds a dead end. There is nothing left. I don't think it is too indicting to say that one who does not rest, in spite of the costs of not doing so, is flinging the gift of the Sabbath in God's face as if there were no value in anything other than one's own productivity. This person would be claiming ownership rather than stewardship of time.

Sabbath practice can be like a detoxification from the poisons of workaholism. Fortunately, when the workaholic's downward spiral is reversed, spirituality is one of the first things recovered. But how do we rest when we are so used to working? How do we stop when there is so much economic, psychological, and emotional momentum pushing us forward?

The Psalmist gives us what may be the best advice: "Trust in the Lord, and do good; so you will live in the land, and enjoy security. Take delight in the Lord, and he will give you the desires of your heart" (Psalm 37:1–4). In other words, practice what gives you joy – then notice how God is present in it. The door through which we enter God's rest and cease from our labours is the door of delight. "…If you call the Sabbath a delight and the holy day of the Lord honorable; if you honor it, not going your own ways, serving your own interests, or pursuing your own affairs; then you shall take delight in the Lord, and I will make you ride upon the heights of the earth…" (Isaiah 58:13, 14).

How do we stop long enough to rest? How do we pause to find out what give us real joy? Not what helps us feel productive, or important, or successful, or powerful, but that which delights our hearts? When we find that thing, be it a playful time with our children, a walk in the woods, cooking a gourmet meal, gardening, or sitting silently in a chair, we find the fingerprints of grace in our lives, and the doorway to true rest and renewal. Through the door of delight we find a spacious, separate, sacred place where our souls are refreshed and life is put back in perspective. The Sabbath place of rest is where we and God take delight in one another. We are reminded that God's delight is not in "the strength of the horse, nor his pleasure in the speed of the runner; but the Lord takes pleasure in those who fear him, in those who hope in his steadfast love" (Psalm147:10–11). "Let us therefore make every effort to enter that rest, so that no one may fall through such disobedience as theirs" (Hebrews 4:11).

For Reflection

Gerald May described addiction as that "which opposes the freedom of love."[11]

> Addictions come from a process that is inherent in the functioning of the cells of our brains and bodies. Psychologically, the process is called conditioning. The spiritual term is attachment. Attachment nails the energy of our passion to someone or something, producing a state of addiction. Once addiction takes hold, the loved one becomes an object to which we are bound. The object of addiction may be anything; a person, a place, a substance, a behavior, a belief. We come to expect gratification from this object and to want more and more of it. Whether we call it dependence or codependence, we have been given away as choicelessly as if sold by a master we never knew existed. Our love, which held such promise of unconditional freedom, has become conditioned and conditional.[12]

Can you name those things or persons you are over-attached to? Allow this prayer to become yours.

Lord God, give peace, for you have given all things to us, the peace of rest, the peace of the Sabbath, the peace without an evening. This entire most beautiful order of things that are very good, when their measure have been accomplished, is to pass away. For truly in them a morning has been made, and an evening also. Then also you shall rest in us, even now as you work in us, and so will that rest of yours be in us, even as these your works are through us. But you, O Lord, are ever at work and ever at rest. You do not see for a time, nor are you moved for a time, nor do you rest for a time. Yet you make both that things be seen in time, and the times themselves, and the rest that comes after time.

AUGUSTINE, CONFESSIONS (4TH CENTURY)[13]

Let us remain as empty as possible so that God can fill us up.

MOTHER TERESA[14]

INTENTION **Today I pray for the grace to loosen my grip on the things, people, and ideas that bring no delight.**

Breath Prayer

BREATHING IN *Delight in the Lord*

BREATHING OUT *with all my heart*

DAY SIX

Review

SABBATH IS ABOUT learning to live "the examined life." That means looking closely at our life and asking if we are going in the direction that leads us toward God's light. This week we held the simplicity of Sabbath in our hearts and minds and asked, "What's important?" When we begin to examine our lives and our world and notice the sky-high levels of depression, illness, and violence, we find that some areas of our lives are out of control, and some of our actions result in massive environmental destruction. As we continue our examination, we see that the well-being of everything on Earth and Earth itself are linked. The lifestyles that are harming us are also harming those we love and the planet we inhabit. We are working too much, consuming too much, and rushing too much. In many cases, we have lost touch with the things that are important, things like community and connection to God and creation.

It is time (*kairos*) to bring Sabbath simplicity into our lives.

FOR REFLECTION

How have you begun to discern the difference between what attracts you on a surface level and what touches the deeper desires of your heart?

Try naming one "thing" that you have spent a great deal of resource on lately. Prayerfully engage in some spiritual archeology to see if there are deeper desires underneath this one major surface desire.

I spend a lot of time and money on _____.

When I sit with my desire for _____, I am able to discern a deeper desire for _____.

As I explore this deeper desire, this is what I discover: _____.

PRAYER

God, only you can satisfy my hungry heart. Help me to spend some time holding the deeper desires of my heart before you. My heart really longs for _____. Help me to receive this gift from you. In Jesus' name, Amen.

INTENTION **Today I bring the deep longings of my heart to the surface.**

BREATH PRAYER

BREATHING IN *As the deer pants for water*

BREATHING OUT *so my soul thirsts for you*

DAY SEVEN

Sabbath Group

OPENING POEM/PRAYER (TOGETHER)

A long
    Loving
        Look at
            The real
                Invites
                    A patient
                        Persistence

So as not
    To avert
        The soul's gaze
            When it is
                Cast upon
                    That which
                        It finds offensive

Prayer like
    God's heart makes
        Room for it all
            Beauty
                Ugliness
                  Freedom
                    Constraint

Do not turn

    Away like children

        In fearful judgment

            Believing that

                Averting prayerful eyes

                    Will magically make

                        Monsters disappear

For it is in

    Courageous

        Compassionate

        Persistence

            That layers of

                Resistance gently

                    Fall away

Stay

    With me

        Abide

      Here

        With me

          Watch and Pray

BREATH PRAYER (TOGETHER)

BREATHING IN *The Lord protects the simple-hearted*

BREATHING OUT *when I was in great need, he saved me*

PSALM 116:6

After two or three minutes of silence the group joins in a song.

Sweep over my Soul.

Sweep over my Soul.

Sweet Spirit, sweep over my Soul.

My rest is complete, as I sit at your feet.

Sweet Spirit sweep over my Soul.[15]

SHARING TIME

Consider and discuss this prayer by St. Augustine.

> Late have I loved you, O Beauty ever ancient, ever new, late have I loved! You were within me, but I was outside, and it was there I searched for you. In my unloveliness I plunged into the lovely things which you created. You were with me, but I was not with you.[16]

How do you feel about the following two statements?

1. Life is what happens when you are planning your life.

2. Joy is what catches you by surprise, from a source that is quite other than where you were pursuing it.

Imagine your relationship with God being like a dance. What is this dance like for you?

THE PRAYER OF EXAMEN

This is a simple prayer exercise that can help us become more attentive to God. It is called the prayer of *examen*, or examination of life. It takes only five or ten minutes, preferably in the evening, and goes like this.

1. Relax in the presence of God. Be aware of God's loving presence in and all around you. Thank God for everything God gives. Name some of the gifts. Ask to be given "the mind and heart of Christ," to see reality as Jesus sees it.

2. Reflect prayerfully over your day, or week, or specific experience. Go through the day with Jesus, checking the "we" (what you and Jesus experienced together) against the "I" (you alone). Jesus lives in us so we can say, as St Paul writes, "I live not for myself alone but Christ lives in me" (Galatians 2:19). This means that in reality your life is a "we" (you and He) not just an "I".

3. As you reflect on the day, notice when you felt a sense of consolation (that is, freedom, lightness, happiness, and gratitude). Also notice the times and circumstances where you felt a kind of desolation (tightness in your chest, a darkness in your heart). For example, I blew up at the kids, I cussed the slow traffic, I got lost in the stress of my world, I judged a friend, I reacted selfishly. As we prayerfully reflect over our day in this way, God sensitizes us to the ways in which the Spirit touches us and is present to us. In other words, God enables us to "discern" or diagnose God's touch from all the other movements and urges in our lives.

4. We call it *examen* because the focus of our attention is on the ways we experience God's loving presence in our daily lives. This focus helps us to become more aware of God's presence and to more peacefully be at work and rest with God in the days to come.

5. Renew in love a sense of sorrow for the times when we move away from God and pray, "Loving God, why do I fear your presence? Yours is an *examen* of love. You know me as I am and love me. Still I am afraid – afraid of what may surface. In this Sabbath pause I invite you to search me to the depths so that I may know myself and you in fuller measure. Amen."[17]

6. If we let God redeem our day and our whole lives in this way, God will. Accept an invitation from God to spend some time alone in quiet, Sabbath prayer tomorrow. Make it a date with a definite place and length of time. Accept any invitation God gives to heal any hurt or change any behaviour the next time we face the kind of situation with which we struggle.

7. End by praying the Lord's Prayer slowly.

If you stick to this prayer period or discernment *examen* for five minutes each day, you will grow your sensitivity to God's presence and be more responsive to God's daily call.

A RESPONSIVE READING

Divide into two groups. The first group reads the odd numbered verses. The second group responds with the even, and the groups join for the last verse.

PSALM 19

1   *The heavens are telling the glory of God; and the firmament proclaims his handiwork.*

2   *Day to day pours forth speech, and night to night declares knowledge.*

3   *There is no speech, nor are there words; their voice is not heard;*

4   *yet their voice goes out through all the earth, and their words to the end of the world. In the heavens he has set a tent for the sun,*

5   *which comes out like a bridegroom from his wedding canopy, and like a strong man runs its course with joy.*

6   *Its rising is from the end of the heavens, and its circuit to the end of them; and nothing is hidden from its heat.*

7   *The law of the Lord is perfect, reviving the soul; the decrees of the Lord are sure, making wise the simple;*

8   *the precepts of the Lord are right, rejoicing the heart; the commandment of the Lord is clear, enlightening the eyes;*

9   *the fear of the Lord is pure, enduring forever; the ordinances of the Lord are true and righteous altogether.*

10   *More to be desired are they than gold, even much fine gold;*
  sweeter also than honey, and drippings of the honeycomb.

11   *Moreover by them is your servant warned; in keeping them there*
  is great reward.

12   *But who can detect their errors? Clear me from hidden faults.*

13   *Keep back your servant also from the insolent; do not let them*
  have dominion over me. Then I shall be blameless, and innocent
  of great transgression.

14   **(ALL) Let the words of my mouth and the meditation of my**
  heart be acceptable to you, O Lord, my rock and my redeemer.

BLESSING (TOGETHER)

**The Lord is near. Let us not worry about anything but in everything
by prayer and supplication with thanksgiving let our requests be
made known to God. And the peace of God, which surpasses all
understanding, will guard our hearts and our minds in Christ
Jesus. Amen. (Philippians 4:5–7)**

Sabbath Is Sacred

God created humankind in his image, in the image
of God did he create it, male and female
did he create them.

GENESIS 1:27

Remember the Sabbath day, and keep it holy.

EXODUS 20:8

HUM*US*ANITY

*Now I know
why "humility"
is rooted in humus.*

*When dancing with the
unsayable it is best
to take off one's shoes;*

*not only out of
respect for the
fire that could consume,*

*but also that you
feel the squishy
dirt between your toes.*

*When gazing through wondrous
mystery it is best to
let words fall to the ground;*

*not only because
of their pale inadequacy
in light of the ineffable,*

*but also that the words
might die in exchange
for the emergence of the fertile new.*

When called to speak
holy things to make us holy
it might be wise to be silent;

not only because what once
felt like truth flowing effortlessly from your lips
now feels like ruminations on mud pie,

but also that out of the soil of unknowing
words of salvation might cleanse
the breath like heavenly mouthwash.

I pray that I and you too
should you choose to join me,
may have the courage

to walk humbly with
God – Earth – Me – You – All
sayable and unsayable

that we may dance
together, barefooted
in the dirt of our humusanity.

DAY ONE

Sanctified

This is the day that the Lord has made;
let us rejoice and be glad in it.

PSALM 118:24

This is the task of men, to conquer space
and sanctify time.

ABRAHAM HESCHEL[1]

THE HEBREW PEOPLE have a greeting they use on the Sabbath day: *Shabbat shalom*, Sabbath peace. It is a greeting that has significant meaning to those who speak it. Although shalom is usually translated as peace, it means far more than a cessation of hostilities, or peace of mind. In the Hebrew language, *shalom* means universal flourishing, wholeness, and delight. *Shalom* describes what a friend of mine calls "the perfection of rightness." It is a state of intimacy with God that gives life meaning and beauty. *Shabbat shalom*, what a wonderful and meaningful greeting. "Good morning, rest in the perfection of rightness." This is the sacred heart of Sabbath, to rest in the wholeness of God and creation.

"Have a great day!" has become the common and trivial greeting in our culture. What might we mean if we meant what we said? What is a great day? What's so significant about this particular day? Great is a word so overused as to be almost meaningless. Stop and think what it may mean for you. Does it mean unlimited, boundless, important, sublime, intense, or maybe outrageous? Or does the greatness of a day have more to do with how much you notice God in it? Would a great day be one in which you accomplish what you set about to do, or one in which you took time to acknowledge who you are?

To sanctify time is to set it aside for a sacred purpose. Sanctified time is time spent preparing to respond to God's invitation to enter God's presence. To sanctify time is to confess that time cannot be conquered or controlled. We can never make more of it. Time flows through our lives like a river. When we sanctify time we learn to swim in this river and not drown.

Sabbath practice creates a special consciousness that recognizes the significance of a day, or a moment in time. Karl Barth recognized the ultimate importance of the seventh day as the time between the creation of the universe, including humankind, and the beginning of humankind's toil and work. Barth says Sabbath is

> God's free, solemn, and joyful satisfaction with that which has taken place and has completed as creation, and His invitation to man to rest with Him, i.e., with Him to be satisfied with that which has taken place through Him. The goal of creation, and at the same time the beginning of all that follows, is the event of God's Sabbath freedom, Sabbath rest and Sabbath joy, in which man, too has been summoned to participate. It is the event of divine rest in the face of the cosmos completed with the creation of man – a rest which takes precedence over all man's eagerness and zeal to enter upon his task. Man is

created to participate in this rest. It is the covenant of the grace of God which in this event, at the supreme and final point of the first creation story, is revealed as the starting point for all that follows. Everything that preceded is the road to this supreme point.[2]

As we work together with him, we urge you also not to accept the grace of God in vain. For he says, "At an acceptable time I have listened to you, and on a day of salvation I have helped you. See now is the acceptable time; see, now is the day of salvation!" (2 Corinthians 6:1–2)

When we practice Sabbath we prepare ourselves for the creative activity that will follow. There is a movement in our lives that happens when we practice Sabbath. I call it the "osmosis effect." Osmosis is the movement of a substance from a region of higher concentration to a region of lower concentration through a semi-permeable membrane so that equilibrium is established. Consider the Holy Spirit as the "substance" that will establish balance in our lives. We know that God's Spirit is omnipresent; everywhere. But when we practice Sabbath we experience a certain intensity of Spirit, a higher concentration of God's presence. However liminal and somewhat fleeting this experience may seem, it is holy, and powerfully transformative. Those who experience the gentle intensity of the Spirit through Sabbath practice will notice how its calming, freeing gifts will flow, almost subversively, through to other places in our life and world.

FOR REFLECTION

But when you pray, go into your room, close the door and pray to your Father, who is unseen. Then your Father, who sees what is done in secret, will reward you.

MATTHEW 6:6

Some homes have an "away room," a library or sitting room for quiet prayer and reading. Where do you go to "get away"? Sometimes entering a sanctified space precedes a sanctified time. What is the place in your home "set apart" for Sabbath reflection? What would you want or need in this space to help facilitate your opening yourself to God (music, books, pictures, a window, a candle)?

The experience of the Holy in Sabbath creates osmosis of Spirit that brings new meaning to all of life and healing to all of creation. One Sabbath morning I reflected on the transformative power of Sabbath and its relationship to the rest of time.

SCENT OF SABBATH

Scent of Sabbath fills the air sweet, fragrant, clean.
As the moments of the day move by there is osmosis of Presence.
It moves from the point of greatest concentration
to that of lesser concentration so that it is
barely distinguishable from ordinary scents
stress, sweat, food, LIFE.

Is the heavenly scent diminished, or merely mixed in to make sacred the ordinary?

INTENTION **Today I prepare a space for God in my outer and inner worlds.**

BREATH PRAYER

BREATHING IN *O Lord, you have searched me*

BREATHING OUT *and you know me*

PSALM 139:1

DAY TWO

Consecrate

*Who then will offer willingly, consecrating
themselves today to the Lord?*

1 CHRONICLES 29:5

I WRITE TODAY'S REFLECTION on the anniversary of 9/11, a day forever etched in our collective memory. I remember the six-month memorial when New York's skyline was consecrated by a girl named Valerie Webb, 12 years old and an orphan. At the appointed time she threw a switch; gradually two soaring towers of light materialized, defiantly piercing the night sky from the wounded western stretch of Lower Manhattan. These luminous ghosts, created by the strategic positioning of 88 high-powered searchlights, were the final tribute in a series of public efforts to remember what hardly had been forgotten. This was a Sabbath moment, a sanctuary in time when we consecrate our memories, our grief, our yearning for peace, and our prayers for the well-being of all our children.

Although closely related to sanctification, consecration takes us one step further into Sabbath. Sanctification (the setting aside of time for the sacred purpose of Sabbath practice) prepares us to respond to God's invitation. Consecration describes our response: we declare something sacred, or dedicate it to divine purpose. To consecrate the Sabbath is to respond to God's invitation to keep Sabbath by intentionally participating with God in rest. To say yes to God's love, we must be willing to enter into that love.

An 18th-century French Jesuit priest referred to "that sacrament of the present moment." In describing his faith he said that everyone could be a saint by simple responsiveness to God's presence in each moment. "There are no moments which are not filled with God's infinite holiness so that there are none we should not honor."[3] During Sabbath moments we turn our hearts toward the Source of Love and offer ourselves, our doubts, our fears, our gratitude, and our desires. In whatever way and to whatever depth we are able, we present ourselves to God as a sacrifice of praise. Paul reminds us of the beauty of this encounter, and that this consecrated offering of our love is "holy and acceptable to God" (Romans 15:16).

In Sabbath moments we realize the fleeting nature of our lives. The writer of Hebrews 13 reminds us, "For here we have no lasting city, but we are looking for the city that is to come. Through him, then, let us continually offer a sacrifice of praise to God, that is, the fruit of lips that confess his name."

After Valerie Webb lit up the sky, two boys stepped forward: Philip Raimondi, 16, and his 12-year-old brother, Peter. Pinned to their lapels was a photograph of their father, Peter F. Raimondi, a vice president for Carr Futures who used to play chess and basketball with them. Philip delivered a short reading, and then Peter approached a lectern that was only slightly shorter than he was. The boy read a poem that ended, "Just around the corner, all is well," and then he was gone.[4]

Sabbath is a consecrated time which helps us to see that "just around the corner, all is well," every manner of thing is well.

FOR REFLECTION

> Moses was keeping the flock of his father-in-law Jethro, the priest of Midian; he led his flock beyond the wilderness, and came to Horeb, the mountain of God. There the angel of the Lord appeared to him in a flame of fire out of a bush; he looked and the bush was blazing, yet it was not consumed. Then Moses said, "I must turn aside and look at this great sight, and see why the bush is not burned up." When the Lord saw that he had turned aside to see, God called to him out of the bush, "Moses, Moses!" And he said, "Here I am." Then he said, "Come no closer! Remove the sandals from your feet, for the place on which you are standing is holy ground." He said further, "I am the God of your father, the God of Abraham, the God of Isaac, and the God of Jacob." And Moses covered his face, for he was afraid to look at God (Exodus 3:1–6).

The dramatic remembrance of 9/11 is not a part of our daily lives. How do we intentionally participate in the divine?

Consider Paul's invitation in Romans 12.

> Therefore, I urge you in view of God's mercy, to offer your bodies as living sacrifices, holy and pleasing to God – this is your spiritual act of worship. Do not conform any longer to the pattern of this world, but be transformed by the renewing of your mind. Then you will be able to test and approve what God's will is – his good, pleasing and perfect will.

Go to your "away" place, close your eyes, and pray.

INTENTION **Today I pause to consider how I "offer myself to God" when I enter the space in which I worship.**

BREATH PRAYER

BREATHING IN *I offer myself*

BREATHING OUT *to you, God*

DAY THREE

Awe

Come and see what God has done: he is awesome in his deeds among mortals.

PSALM 66:5

When the crowds saw it, they were filled with awe, and they glorified God, who had given such authority to human beings.

MATTHEW 9:8

ONE THING THAT set Jesus apart from other teachers of his time was the authority he taught with. His teaching filled people with awe. Awe is a wonderful, albeit oft-forgotten emotion, and one which seems especially elusive.

Several years ago I sat with my mother in a Starbucks coffee shop talking about life and death. This was no abstract or hypothetical discussion. Mom had just received a diagnosis of multiple myeloma, an incurable cancer that affects the plasma cells in the blood. We sensed awe, dread, and wonder as we spoke of her feelings of hope and fear, trust and doubt. As we spoke we were gifted with a Sabbath moment. (You realize by now that Sabbath moments stretch far beyond our scheduled prayer times and can happen when we least expect it.) There was a feeling of awe-full holiness that settled over us. The dread was not one that caused our chests to tighten in fear. The wonder was not full of nagging questions. Rather, an ineffable presence filled our hearts as we sat in reverential silence for several minutes. We journeyed together after that time knowing that when death came we would be better prepared to meet it.

Awe is the feeling you get when you stand on the edge of the Grand Canyon. As I stood on the South Rim I was filled with awe, whelmed (not overwhelmed!) by the beauty of God's creation, humbled as I considered my smallness. That was the feeling of wonder. I'm sure glad there was a fence because there was a certain dread that found its way deep into my stomach imagining that there was some force that would push or pull me into the depths if I wasn't careful.

Karl Rahner is credited with the statement that, "The time is fast approaching when one will either be a mystic or an unbeliever."[5] In today's agnostic, materialistic, technological culture, there is danger that awe is becoming an extinct emotion. If you choose to hang out in Sabbath space for long, resting in the presence of God, you may find a sense of awe rise up from within. Receive this as a Sabbath gift and offer it back to God as praise.

For Reflection

Practice *lectio divina* with the following passage. (See page 75 for a description of the practice.)

> O Lord, our Lord, how majestic is your name in all the earth! You have set your glory above the heavens. From the lips of children and infants you have ordained praise because of your enemies, to silence the foe and the avenger. When I consider your heavens, the work of your fingers, the moon and the stars, which you have set in place, what is man that you are mindful

of him, the son of man that you care for him? You made him
a little lower than the heavenly beings and crowned him with
glory and honor. You made him ruler over the works of your
hands; you put everything under his feet: all flocks and herds,
and the beasts of the field, the birds of the air, and the fish of
the sea, all that swim the paths of the seas. O Lord, our Lord,
how majestic is your name in all the earth! (Psalm 8)

INTENTION ***Today I stand in awe of God's presence in the world.***

BREATH PRAYER

BREATHING IN *God*

BREATHING OUT *Wow*

DAY 4

Sanctuary

I will lie down and sleep in peace, for you alone, O
Lord, make me dwell in safety.

PSALM 4:8

So again Jesus said to them, "Very truly, I tell you,
I am the gate for the sheep. All who came before me
are thieves and bandits; but the sheep did not listen
to them. I am the gate. Whoever enters by me will
be saved (or kept safe), and will come in and go out
and find pasture. The thief comes only to steal and
kill and destroy. I came that they may have life, and
have it abundantly."

JOHN 10:7–10

B Y NOW YOU are becoming familiar with Sabbath's varied
landscape. Have you been surprised by any of your discoveries?
Seasoned travellers know that rarely does a newly explored land match
one's preconceived ideas of what the unexplored, inexperienced territory
is like. For the spiritual tourist this can feel like disappointment. Those
who have misconceived notions that Sabbath is something that can be

accomplished, defined, or contained, or that it will always be peaceful, will begin sensing an increasing, perhaps intolerable, frustration or disappointment. They may not feel safe. Threatened by the unknown, this is as far as some may choose to go. Others who are less like tourists and more like pilgrims also sense frustration and disappointment. However, because they have embraced the unfolding, dynamic nature of the Sabbath journey, the sense of adventure continues to grow. They are able to hold the restlessness that accompanies continuing Sabbath practice. A desire for more Sabbath experience ferments. What new discoveries await us further down the Sabbath path?

The deeper you go into Sabbath territory the more likely you are to encounter a strange sense of dis-ease or disequilibrium. Accompanying this feeling of being off-balance is an intuitive sense that the discomfort is one that will lead to greater life and freedom. Notice how this feeling is different than the feeling of dis-ease you encountered as you began the journey. You are discovering that some of the ways you have been living in time no longer make sense. This realization points to the transitional nature of the Sabbath journey.

There is one essential knowing that the Sabbath pilgrim must have in order to continue any further on this journey. You must know you are safe. The assurance of safety will not be present instantly but must rather be prayerfully kindled like a fire on a dark, windy night. A growing awareness that here, in this Sabbath space, where you have placed your trust in God the Creator of heaven and earth and not in your own capacities, you are perfectly safe.

> Can a woman forget her nursing-child, or show no compassion
> for the child of her womb? Even these may forget, yet I will
> not forget you. See, I have inscribed you on the palms of my
> hands; your walls are continually before me (Isaiah 49:15–16).

Those who continue practicing Sabbath will experience Sabbath as a "holding environment" or "sanctuary in time." It is only from a place of safety that one finds the clues or the signposts that point to new beginnings. Now you are ready to bring more of the wisdom you have gained and the new rhythms of living you have discovered back "home" into the everyday reality of your life. Time spent in Sabbath has begun its spiritual alchemy.

FOR REFLECTION

Remember going on a trip as a child. What feelings of expectations did you have as you prepared for the trip? How did those expectations connect to your actual experience?

Can you remember the expectations you had for this Sabbath Journey? What surprises have you encountered?

Ponder these words: "Sabbath is an antidote to the enormous anxiety we have about the fragility of the world" (Walter Brueggemann, *Talking about Genesis: A Resource Guide*).

Practice *lectio divina: lectio, meditatio, oratio, contemplatio.*

> The Lord is my shepherd, I shall not want. He makes me lie down in green pastures; he leads me beside still waters; he restores my soul. He leads me in right paths for his name's sake. Even though I walk through the darkest valley, I fear no evil; for you are with me; your rod and your staff – they comfort me. You prepare a table before me in the presence of my enemies; you anoint my head with oil; my cup overflows. Surely goodness and mercy shall follow me all the days of my life, and I shall dwell in the house of the Lord my whole life long (Psalm 23).

INTENTION **Today I rest in the knowledge that I am perfectly safe in God's Sabbath.**

BREATH PRAYER

BREATHING IN *I will fear no evil*

BREATHING OUT *for you are with me*

Ritual

As they came near the village to which they were going, he walked ahead as if he were going on. But they urged him strongly, saying, "Stay with us, because it is almost evening and the day is now nearly over." So he went in to stay with them. When he was at the table with them, he took bread, blessed and broke it, and gave it to them. Then their eyes were opened, and they recognized him; and he vanished from their sight.

LUKE 24:28–31

We have lost a sense of Sabbath in our lives – a sense of joy and delight, a sense of what we do when we come face to face with mystery of existence itself.

MATTHEW FOX[6]

MANY "ISMS" CHARACTERIZE our postmodern world. Consumerism, individualism, materialism, and workaholism are symptoms that, if acknowledged, draw our attention to the restlessness of life. They are symptoms of a chronic chronological dis-ease. Sabbath is an opportunity to transform these "isms" into a more holy way of living. We have learned that Sabbath practice moves us from one way of living to another. It helps us become aware of the suffering caused by swearing allegiance to the god of *chronos*.

Sabbath ritual can help us negotiate with these powers of *chronos*. Rather than just getting mad as hell or, worse, ignoring the symptoms, ritual is a way of meeting the suffering head on. Ritual is a part of everyday life in those parts of the world where physical suffering is encountered on a regular basis. Some suffering is just too difficult to approach directly. A ritual can create a caricature of the suffering so that it can be looked at and transformed into a life-giving experience. From ritualistic dances in so called "developing" countries, to the slave songs of recent American history, indigenous rituals help people face the reality of suffering and channel its destructive energies into those that give life. There are many rituals in our lives. Most major life transitions are accompanied by rituals. These rituals serve as markers and help us to face experiences that can be too overwhelming to face naked, unmasked, head on.

Consider the rituals that are a part of Christian liturgy. Christians regularly share bread and wine as reminders of Christ's broken body and shed blood. As we partake of the bread and wine we are brought face to face with an incomprehensible suffering. Yet we know these means of grace are meant to bring us into wholeness. The broken body becomes a source of healing. The shed blood is transfigured into the cup of salvation. A special meal, Sabbath candles, a solitary walk in the woods, or just a quiet togetherness are rituals that can help us face the symptoms of our present suffering and transfigure the experiences into expressions of the world to come. As you move deeper into Sabbath practice, you are invited to find rituals that help guide you, or to create your own rituals.

FOR REFLECTION

In this text from Romans 8:18–27, Paul speaks of a groaning so deep that it is heard in all of creation. Could it be that creation (including you and me) groans because we are out of step with God's time?

I consider that the sufferings of this present time are not worth comparing with the glory about to be revealed to us. For the creation waits with eager longing for the revealing of the children of God; for the creation was subjected to futility, not of its own will but by the will of the one who subjected it, in hope that the creation itself will be set free from its bondage to decay and will obtain the freedom of the glory of the children of God. We know that the whole creation has been groaning in labour pains until now; and not only the creation, but we ourselves, who have the first fruits of the Spirit, groan inwardly while we wait for adoption, the redemption of our bodies. For in hope we were saved. Now hope that is seen is not hope. For who hopes for what is seen? But if we hope for what we do not see, we wait for it with patience.

Likewise the Spirit helps us in our weakness; for we do not know how to pray as we ought, but that very Spirit intercedes with sighs too deep for words. And God, who searches the heart, knows what is the mind of the Spirit, because the Spirit intercedes for the saints according to the will of God.

What are the "present sufferings" in your life? What rituals could you create to help you transform the suffering in your life?

INTENTION ***Today I will create a simple ritual to help me name and transform my restlessness.***

Breath Prayer

BREATHING IN *If God is for us,*

BREATHING OUT *who is against us*

ROMANS 8:31

Review

Thus says the Lord: Maintain justice, and do what is right, for soon my salvation will come, and my deliverance be revealed. Happy is the mortal who does this, the one who holds it fast, who keeps the sabbath, not profaning it, and refrains from doing any evil. Do not let the foreigner joined to the Lord say, "The Lord will surely separate me from his people"; and do not let the eunuch say, "I am just a dry tree." For thus says the Lord: To the eunuchs who keep my sabbaths, who choose the things that please me and hold fast my covenant, I will give, in my house and within my walls, a monument and a name better than sons and daughters; I will give them an everlasting name that shall not be cut off. And the foreigners who join themselves to the Lord, to minister to him, to love the name of the Lord, and to be his servants, all who keep the sabbath, and do not profane it, and hold fast my covenant – these I will bring to my holy mountain, and make them joyful in my house of prayer; their burnt-offerings

and their sacrifices will be accepted on my altar; for
my house shall be called a house of prayer for all
peoples. Thus says the Lord God, who gathers the
outcasts of Israel, I will gather others to them besides
those already gathered.

ISAIAH 56:1–8

THIS WEEK WE have explored the dimensions of the sacred heart of the Sabbath and learned how we must prepare ourselves to enter its healing chambers.

None of us are natives to this Sabbath territory we have been exploring for these five weeks. All of us are strangers in the land. Yet God has named God's house "a house of prayer for all nations." This house is holy. It is sacred.

But just as in the days of Israel's exile and return, God's house can be desecrated. When we forget that the Sabbath is a sacred time and place and take lightly the Sabbath command, we shut ourselves out in the cold.

FOR REFLECTION

Vini sancta spiritus, Come, Holy Spirit. This is the prayer for opening the door to God so that our space may be filled with God. Try praying this prayer as often as you can today.

Let the words of this poem lead you along the Sabbath path.

HOW THE QUESTION CHANGES

what can be compared
to the movement from
the centre of my perceived
security into the
mystery of Life's beckoning call?

is it like

seed scooped
from the silo
by the farmer's
giant calloused hand
ready to be broadcast
over varied soil?

is it like

the Monet painting
First Steps
with child stumbling
across lush garden into
her father's outstretched
and longing arms?

is it like

Peter's clumsy misadventure
leaping into a watery confusion
of faith and presumption
and sinking like the rock
after which he is named?

is it like

a free-fall from
6,000 feet
tethered to the
one who has taken
this reckless leap
before and lived on?

Is it like

an adoption gone wrong
the bonded toddler
being pried from
the arms of the only
guardian he ever knew and
placed by the social worker
into the arms of a stranger?

is it like

the cold naked November day
standing beside my mother's grave
taking a grasp of dirt from underneath
the Astroturf meant to soften
death's starkness
casting it onto casket's lid?

and now on the Sabbath path
as my heart opens and I let go
into the sacred place of transformation
where the holy seeps into the ordinary
the question changes from
What is it like?
to
How can I keep from singing?

INTENTION ***Today I find rest in my Sabbath home.***

BREATH PRAYER

BREATHING IN *Holy Spirit*

BREATHING OUT *come to me*

Sabbath Group

OPENING PRAYER (TOGETHER)

Like the prophet Isaiah we can say, "I saw the Lord seated on a throne, high and exalted, and the train of his robe filled the temple." We are humbled by your holiness and hushed by your majesty. Into this sacred silence you reach out and lift us up that we may continue on the Sabbath Journey. Guide us in our intention to walk with you and with each other on this path you have set before us. Help us to know that we are safe so we can let down our guard and trust.

Leader: This week we have experienced the sacredness of Sabbath. We have experienced the Holy. Today we are reminded that we are not alone on this journey but share in community.

BREATH PRAYER

BREATHING IN *Come Holy Spirit*

BREATHING OUT *fill us with your love*

After two or three minutes of silence, the group joins in chanting the breath prayer: Come Holy Spirit, fill us with your love.

SHARING TIME

What are the ways you notice the Holy in your life experience?

How do you prepare for prayer (externally and/or internally)?

Awe is described as being a combination of dread and wonder. Can you remember an experience of awe?

"I know God will not give me anything I can't handle. I just wish that He didn't trust me so much." Mother Teresa[7]

CLOSING

BLESSING (TOGETHER)

The Lord is near. Let us not worry about anything but in everything by prayer and supplication with thanksgiving let our requests be made known to God. And the peace of God, which surpasses all understanding, will guard our hearts and our minds in Christ Jesus. Amen. (Philippians 4:5–7)

WEEK SIX

Continuing

*Thus were finished the heavens and the earth,
with all of their array. God had finished, on the
seventh day, his work that he had made, and then
he ceased, on the seventh day, from all his work
that he had made.*[1]

GENESIS 2:1–2

LIFE IS ENOUGH

Finding comfort in
holding a loaf of bread, like
a child enduring
the London bombings,

the farmer kneels before
summer's field, stale bread
in hand, waiting for the earth
to bring her bounty.

In this sheer silence
there is nothing
to do but watch
and wait
and remember.

It was not without an
early spring sweat that
layers of fallow ground
were peeled back

to uncover hitherto
unknown parts,
and open dark places
to the sun's gift.

From whence does
the courage and wisdom
come for this great
kenotic act?

What foolish wisdom
is embedded in the
sower's heart that
yields to this death before life?

It is memory
residing in the
God-imaged cells that
makes the sowing possible.

The tiller breathes deeply
Summer's sweet aroma,
a teasing anticipation
of the coming Sabbath feast.

For surely,
as in days gone by,
Autumn will bring her promised gifts
to the table.

Fruited wine, earthy bread
will weigh the farmer's
board with a
celebration of abundance.

With the whole household
gathered round
a blessing is given
in gratitude that life is enough.

DAY 1

Horizon

I have told you these things, so that in me you
may have peace. In this world you will have trouble.
But take heart! I have overcome the world.

JOHN 14:27

Peace I leave with you; my peace I give you. I do not
give to you as the world gives. Do not let your hearts
be troubled and do not be afraid.

JOHN 16:33

AT FIRST, JESUS' promise of holy disruption seems at odds with his teachings of peace. Yet this is a paradox that we are wise to embrace. We expect increasing peace in our continuing practice. After all, Sabbath is the practice of peace. It is inherently restful. It is the fertile ground from which peace that passes understanding grows. What surprises us is the simultaneous experience of increasing restlessness. The more we experience Sabbath rest the more we become sensitized to a restlessness that is inherent in all people, perhaps in all creation. This restless longing is as powerful as it is ubiquitous, and whether this restlessness leads us toward God or away from God depends on our willingness to be aware of it, hold it, and focus it so that it leads us forward toward an infinite horizon.

We started our Sabbath practice by reflecting on the fact that we are created in the image of God *(imago Dei)*. There is something of God in every person. To put this truth in postmodern slang, we might say we got soul! Soul is that part of us that is in the image of God. It is what gives us life; it is what draws us toward God and one another. It is the fire within, the pulse of life (some call this *eros*, or energy that longs for love). It is the source of our longing and the spark of our restlessness.

We're cracked pots, leaky urns, incapable of containing the treasure God poured in when God first breathed life into us. We simply cannot contain all that God desires for us. We notice this when beauty makes us restless when it could bring us peace; when the love we experience with another doesn't quite satisfy; or when where we are seems boring.

Here is where trust in God's continuing ability to fill our leaky lives with grace grows. Do not lose heart. God will continue to pour life into us. For now, just be aware of the mystery of the Sabbath paradox of peace and holy disruption.

> Therefore we do not lose heart. Though outwardly we are wasting away, yet inwardly we are being renewed day by day. For our light and momentary troubles are achieving for us an eternal glory that far outweighs them all. So we fix our eyes not on what is seen, but on what is unseen. For what is seen is temporary, but what is unseen is eternal (2 Corinthians 4:16–18).

I have a young friend, who, near the beginning of his Sabbath practice, asked me what the point of a question was if not to find an answer. My response to him was in part the following.

> If you find that there are questions that keep surfacing and elude attempts to either answer them or ignore them, then it is, I think, best to find ways to "be" with them; ways that lead to more life, more curiosity, more adventure, increasing clarity, and even some peace. What generally happens, however, is that

people do their best to ignore the restlessness stirred up by these persistent questions, or try to satisfy them in ways that only make things worse: taking drugs; drinking; shopping; indulging in dysfunctional relationships; or, the biggest escape of all, embracing fundamentalism of any kind.

Saint Augustine famously said, "God, you have made us for yourself and our hearts remain restless until they find rest in thee." We are meant to live with longing, and to move toward a fulfillment of that longing. Our restless longing reminds us that we are living and, at our best, loving.

INTENTION **Today I hold gently my inner restlessness, knowing that it is the Spirit at work.**

BREATH PRAYER

BREATHING IN *Wind of God*

BREATHING OUT *blow strongly in me*

Lament

Now I rejoice, not because you were grieved, but because your grief led to repentance; for you felt a godly grief, so that you were not harmed in any way by us. For godly grief produces a repentance that leads to salvation and brings no regret, but worldly grief produces death. For see what earnestness this godly grief has produced in you, what eagerness to clear yourselves, what indignation, what alarm, what longing, what zeal, what punishment! At every point you have proved yourselves guiltless in the matter.

2 CORINTHIANS 7:9–11

AS WE HOLD together in that Sabbath place in our hearts both the increasing desire for peace, and the restlessness that has surfaced, a certain sorrow begins to emerge. At some point, we realize that we will not arrive at a place of perfection or completion. Our dream of a final fulfillment, our longing for full rest, our thirst for never-ending peace will remain unfulfilled for as long as we live. This is an "awe-full" but necessary discovery.

There is a necessary discipline that we must learn in order to live in this tension between longing and the lack of consummation. It is the spiritual discipline of lament. The Bible offers a powerful and disturbing archetypical story to teach us of this spiritual task. Despite its cruel and patriarchal context, there is a powerful lesson to learn in the story of Jephthah in Judges 11.

Then the spirit of the Lord came upon Jephthah, and he passed through Gilead and Manasseh. He passed on to Mizpah of Gilead, and from Mizpah of Gilead he passed on to the Ammonites. And Jephthah made a vow to the Lord, and said, "If you will give the Ammonites into my hand, then whoever comes out of the doors of my house to meet me, when I return victorious from the Ammonites, shall be the Lord's, to be offered up by me as a burnt-offering." So Jephthah crossed over to the Ammonites to fight against them; and the Lord gave them into his hand. He inflicted a massive defeat on them from Aroer to the neighbourhood of Minnith, twenty towns, and as far as Abel-keramim. So the Ammonites were subdued before the people of Israel.

Then Jephthah came to his home at Mizpah; and there was his daughter coming out to meet him with timbrels and with dancing. She was his only child; he had no son or daughter except her. When he saw her, he tore his clothes, and said, "Alas, my daughter! You have brought me very low; you have become the cause of great trouble to me. For I have opened my mouth to the Lord, and I cannot take back my vow." She said to him, "My father, if you have opened your mouth to the Lord, do to me according to what has gone out of your mouth, now that the Lord has given you vengeance against your enemies, the Ammonites." And she said to her father, "Let this thing be done for me: Grant me two months, so that I may go and wander on the mountains, and bewail my virginity, my companions and I." "Go," he said and sent her away for two months. So she departed, she and her companions, and bewailed her virginity on the mountains. At the end of two months, she returned to her father, who did with her according to the vow he had made.

In a very real way, the Sabbath journey leads us into the desert places where we must mourn our "virginity" and come to terms with our dissatisfaction and incompleteness. In the end we all die incomplete, an unfinished symphony.[2] If we fail to allow our hearts to lament, if we do not grieve our incompleteness, our restlessness will turn to bitterness, our longing to gnawing disappointment, our delight to disillusionment. We will then continue to seek satisfaction in ways that become manipulative and destructive. Sabbath practice will contain many little deaths and resurrections. Learning to live with these movements will keep us open to God.

FOR REFLECTION

I was at ease in everything to be sure, but at the same time satisfied with nothing. Each joy made me desire another. I went from festivity to festivity. On one occasion I danced for nights on end, ever madder about people and life. At times, late on those nights when dancing, the slight intoxication, my wild enthusiasm, everyone's violent unrestraint would fill me with a tired and overwhelming rapture, it would seem to me – that at last I understood the secret creatures of the world. But my fatigue would disappear the next day, and with it the secret . . .

Because I longed for eternal life, I went to bed with harlots and drank for nights on end.

ALBERT CAMUS [3]

You are so young, so before all beginning, and I want to beg you, as much as I can, dear sir, to be patient toward all that is unsolved in your heart and to try to love the questions themselves like locked rooms and like books that are written in a very foreign tongue. Do not seek the answers, which cannot be given you because you would not be able to look at them. And the point is, to live everything. Live the questions now.

RAINER MARIA RILKE [4]

Come, let us return to the Lord;

for it is he who has torn, and he will heal us;

he has struck down, and he will bind us up.

After two days he will revive us;

on the third day he will raise us up,

that we may live before him.

Let us know, let us press on to know the Lord;

his appearing is as sure as the dawn;

he will come to us like the showers,

like the spring rains that water the earth.

HOSEA 6: 1–3

A poem written in the moments after my father's death.

DUST

Through the tears and
Raspy breath and the
Letting go, not in the
Metaphorical sense,
It all seems like dust.

all dust

The words and the
Freight they carry;
The plans and aspirations;
Accumulated wisdom, or that
Which you counted as such;
Someone else's faith that
Never quite fit the contours
Of your heart; prayers too.

dust

Yet there is a memory
Or was it a dream or
Premonition of
When dust rises from

The earth and meets
Creator's breath
And begins to dance.

Is all this dust the same
Being reshaped over
And over through eternity
Into a father or son,
A star or a rose
Which lives and dies
Until the next resurrection?

INTENTION **Today I feel the sorrow that comes with the realization that in this life I will continue to be restless and thirst for more.**

BREATH PRAYER

BREATHING IN *Wait for the Lord*

BREATHING OUT *who renews my strength*

BASED ON ISAIAH 40:31

DAY THREE

Imagination

Thus says the Lord, who makes a way in the sea, a path in the mighty waters, who brings out chariot and horse, army and warrior; they lie down, they cannot rise, they are extinguished, quenched like a wick: Do not remember the former things, or consider the things of old. I am about to do a new thing; now it springs forth, do you not perceive it? I will make a way in the wilderness and rivers in the desert. The wild animals will honour me, the jackals and the ostriches; for I give water in the wilderness, rivers in the desert, to give drink to my chosen people, the people whom I formed for myself so that they might declare my praise.

ISAIAH 43:16–21

Knowledge is limited. Imagination encircles the world.

ALBERT EINSTEIN[5]

A S WE HAVE seen, it takes much courage, perseverance, and patience to look into our hearts. Sometimes we are disturbed by what we find. Fears, loneliness, and our culture's fixation with materialism leave us feeling more than disquieted. The shadows of greed, lust, and selfishness stir in us a hunger for God's healing touch.

Sabbath is an opportunity to look at the internal realities of our lives. It is also an opportunity to look at the realities of the world around us. As we begin to see all of life against the infinite horizon of God's love, our compassion swells for those in our world who suffer.

Against this background, Sabbath invites us to trust God and to acknowledge that we cannot save ourselves or our world. Here we are free to hope in God's future. Letting go of the paralyzing myth that we can actually fix it all leaves us free to imagine what God can do. And God can do amazing things!

When Isaiah delivered the promise of "water in the desert" the people of Israel were languishing in foreign exile. Think of how their imaginations must have been stirred when they heard the words of the prophet. The imagination has been called the highest power of the knowing mind. It is the power by which we sort and shape all the disparate elements of our world by using images, symbols, stories, and rituals. As we seek to find meaning and purpose for our lives, it helps to nurture a habit of imagination.

I'm not saying we should live in a fantasy world. I think it can be helpful to have an active fantasy life. Fantasy can keep the mind open and limber; it can entertain; it can be a means of experimenting. But the problem with fantasy is that it need have no relationship to reality and can lead to its own seductive pleasure or horror. Imagination incorporates fantasy, but its highest function is to create the real.

The four authors of a helpful book titled *Common Fire: Leading Lives of Commitment in a Complex World* conducted a study of 100 people who had made a significant commitment to the common good. They found that one thing these people had in common was the capacity to imagine. The authors also noticed a regular pattern of progression in their imaginative work.

A starting point was being conscious of *conflict*. Something not right, dissonant. What is won't work. This disturbance in the status quo was followed by an intentional *pause*. For the Sabbath pilgrim, this pause is prayer; a long, loving look at the real.

Out of this fruitful pause an *image* (not necessarily visual) or *insight* emerges. The gift of the pause is the *ah-ha*! It has been my experience that the images of prayer take the form at least initially of metaphor.

Once a new image of what can be is found, a connection between the new insight and lived experience is sought. The authors call this *re-patterning and refraining*. Somehow the *ah-ha* needs to be shaped into our lives. And if the new thing is to live in the world, it needs to be articulated and acted upon in *community* with other people who are interested. As the authors put it, "We are dependent on trustworthy communities of confirmation and contradiction who can affirm that, 'Yes, life is like that' or respond, 'No, that interpretation is inadequate, perhaps even dangerous.'"[6]

I believe imagining a new "world" is a primary task of the church. Could this be a model for evangelism, to let the words of Scripture and our tradition be the fuel for our imaginations? From the perspective of our faith and our experiences of the Holy, we can begin to notice "conscious conflict" – the brokenness and contradiction. We can notice what is, so that we can imagine what could be. We could take time to pray, to pause, reflect, wonder, wait, and discern. Sabbath is the atmosphere where this sort of prayer can thrive and allow God's Holy Spirit to stir within us the *ah-ha*, the new thing. In the free and spacious geography of Sabbath we can faithfully interpret that new thing so that it can have relevance for our lives. And we are able to test what we have imagined in the context of Christian community.

FOR REFLECTION

You might ask, "How can I have an open mind when I just cannot imagine agreeing with the other point of view?"

The substance of an "idea," its "rightness" or "wrongness," and the degree to which you are convinced of its "truth," matter less on the journey of transformation than the way in which the idea is held in your mind/heart. In order for progress to be made, the ideas, no matter how firmly planted in our minds, need to be held lightly, with epistemological humility that makes room for the other. One need not agree with the other, or let go of one's convictions. But in order for the future to emerge, one must learn how to have a posture of openness. As scary as that may seem, the alternative is truly devastating. So maybe it's not so much changing one's mind as it is opening oneself to the possibility of change.

THERE'S A PART OF ME

There's a part of me
that wants to be heard
that wants to share with
others a few nuggets of gold
I've found amongst the craggy
cliffs of my curiosity.

I can still remember
the thrill of discovery
when as a child I found
a vein of gold in the woods
behind the house.

In an instant whole
new worlds opened up in my
imagination as all boundaries
and limits dissolved in the
shimmering light of my discovery.

But as quickly as the road,
yellow with bricks of gold,
appeared before me
the thin filigree of pure innocence
was washed away by reality's rain.

It seems the treasure
of my dreams
was that of a fool
tricked by pyrite's* metallic lustre.
I didn't audition for the part of the fool.

But even as some childlike
innocence was purified
to make way for the real,
some wound remained
even to this day.

There's a part of me
yes, it's foolish I know
that still believes that what I found
in the woods behind my house
is real and will pave the Way home.

*Pyrite, fool's gold - πυρίτης (Greek puritēs – of fire)

INTENTION **Today I dream the impossible dream.**

BREATH PRAYER

BREATHING IN *God calls that which is not*

BREATHING OUT *as though it is*

DAY FOUR

Fidelity

Jesus said to him, "No one who puts a hand to the plough and looks back is fit for the kingdom of God."

LUKE 9:62

My heart is steadfast, O God, my heart is steadfast. I will sing and make melody. Awake, my soul! Awake, O harp and lyre! I will awake the dawn.

PSALM 57:7–8

A LONG THE WAY, we can find ourselves lost, unmotivated, confused, or just plain tired. How can we continue our Sabbath practice? There is no end in sight. So in order to carry on, we need to acknowledge that we are not called to finish the race or to win the battle, but to remain faithful to the practice.

To sustain ourselves as we continue on the Sabbath journey we need to remind ourselves that it is not about winning or losing but about fidelity. It is not about getting there but about being here. It is not about success but faithfulness. There are many times when we just don't know which way to go or how to proceed. There are plenty of occasions when prayer lacks inspiration. Motivation wanes. What do we do? We just show up.

By now a daily rhythm of prayer has begun to root itself deeper in your life. Sabbath is becoming a way of life that makes sense. Even when it seems like you are doing the same old thing, and Sabbath practice is boring and tiresome – and especially when God feels distant and your heart empty – moments of intentional rest provide new invitations for greater freedom and deeper love.

Sabbath opens our hearts to hope. Practicing Sabbath is the practice of participative, prayerful hope, hope to which you are committed, and hope which you have given yourself.

FOR REFLECTION

Blessing covers the dry land like a river, and drenches it like a flood.

SIRACH 39:22

Each new day
before setting out
on the sun scorched path
I pause by the well
fed by love's stream
to fill my soul's reservoir
with Sabbath's essential blessing.
Into a dry and weary land
I carry the canteen of commitment
from which I shall draw
when faced with
long spells of rejection
and if by chance or
seduced by some mirage
I find myself lost

in a parched place
I will turn once more
to my canteen, now a grail
to be refreshed for the
journey home.

INTENTION **In the Sabbath pause I find rest, strength, and courage for the journey.**

BREATH PRAYER

BREATHING IN *My heart is ready*

BREATHING OUT *I mean to sing and play for you*

DAY FIVE

Gratitude

O come, let us sing to the Lord;

let us make a joyful noise to the rock of our salvation!

Let us come into his presence with thanksgiving;

let us make a joyful noise to him with songs of praise!

For the Lord is a great God,

and a great King above all gods.

In his hand are the depths of the earth;

the heights of the mountains are his also.

The sea is his, for he made it,

and the dry land, which his hands have formed.

PSALM 95:1–5

I awoke this morning with devout thanksgiving for
my friends, the old and the new. Shall I not call
God the Beautiful, who daily showeth himself
so to me in his gifts?

RALPH WALDO EMERSON[7]

WHEN WE BECOME tired or even exhausted, there is a deep well of refreshment that awaits us. The water in that well is gratitude. Stop along the way and lower your heart's vessel into the well. You will find that gratitude opens your heart to God's ever-present love. Negativity, fear, anger, and jealousy are soothed by the waters of gratitude. Your heart becomes open to God's love and you experience the joy and depth of just being. No wonder Saint Paul urges us to "rejoice always" and to "give thanks in all circumstances" (Philippians 4:4).

Like other Sabbath gifts, gratitude can be cultivated. We can develop gratitude by noticing what is. This is why Sabbath practice is so conducive to developing the gift of gratitude. Sabbath invites pausing and noticing.

Like most parents I remind my children to be thankful for all God's blessings. The practice or discipline of gratitude can be exercised in the midst of life's most challenging or most ordinary moments. But sometimes gratitude comes to us as pure gift, unexpected and surprising. Sometimes the way to gratitude is not through intention or willfulness, but through dying to all our efforts, through letting go. When we stop long enough to experience the life all around us, we can find ourselves actually carried away by gratitude. This poem that I wrote after a morning walk at a local state park describes such an experience of gratitude.

A SABBATH BRIDE

I felt I was a guest at a great wedding
then discovered it was
I who was being wed.
I was a bride betrothed to
the Mystery.

There was no silken white runner
no candles on the altar
no scripture or rings
no Pachelbel's Canon
or distant relatives there
mostly for the reception.

Only the sandy path
bounded on each side
by cranberry bogs
like pews on which sat
the Canada geese
friends of both bride and groom.

The bright blue Smooth Asters –
Symphyotrichum laeve –
stood witness in all their
autumn glory.

Barn swallows danced
to some silent song
that could not be found
in the DJ's collection.

I stood in amazement
taking the world into my arms
met there at Nature's altar
by the I Am
all that I said was
"I do!"

FOR REFLECTION

The poet David Whyte asked Brother David Steindl-Rast to reflect on exhaustion.

> Let go of all this effort, and let yourself down, however awkwardly, into the waters of the work you want for yourself. It's all right, you know, to support yourself with something secondary until your work has ripened, but once it has ripened to a transparent fullness, it has to be gathered in. You have ripened already, and you are waiting to be brought in. Your exhaustion is a form of inner fermentation. You are beginning, ever so slowly...to rot on the vine.[8]

"Rot on the vine." What an image. The longer we avoid stopping at the wells of gratitude the more likely we are to rot, wither, and die. Why not stop right now and drink deeply of gratitude?

INTENTION **Today I am grateful for the gift of gratitude.**

BREATH PRAYER

BREATHING IN *Let my heart*

BREATHING OUT *overflow with thankfulness*

COLOSSIANS 2:7

DAY SIX

Blessing

God saw everything that he had made,
and indeed, it was very good.

GENESIS 1:31

The one who testifies to these things says,
"Surely I am coming soon."
Amen. Come, Lord Jesus! The grace of the
Lord Jesus be with all the saints. Amen.

REVELATION 22:20–21

THE BIBLE BEGINS and ends with a blessing. Sure, there's a lot of life, death, and resurrection in the pages between the covers but still, from alpha to omega, from Genesis to Revelation, from the beginning of time to its end, blessing prevails. Remember the definition of Sabbath at the beginning of this resource? In essence, Sabbath is a safe place at the heart of creation. It is an environment where we are invited to practice a non-anxious presence that we may learn to live into the reality of God's essential blessing.

The word blessing takes its root from the Latin verb *benedicere*, to speak well of. To bless someone is to speak well of him or her, to say what is most true of that person. To bless is to name and affirm the essential nature of a person or being. When Jesus says, "Blessed are the poor in spirit for theirs is the kingdom of Heaven," he is not defining their essential nature as "the poor." Rather Jesus points to a greater, more permanent reality: he names them as people belonging to God's kingdom. Once again I am reminded of Rilke's words, "My life is not this steeply sloping hour, in which you see me hurrying."[9]

We are essentially blessed with God's love. "Just to be is a blessing. Just to live is holy," wrote Rabbi Abraham Heschel.[10] The problem is, many of us don't seem to believe this. Do you? Is the God you worship the God who takes delight in you, not because of what you have achieved or will accomplish, but because of your essential nature as God's beloved creation? Julian of Norwich celebrates the delight God takes in us with these words: "God sits in heaven smiling, completely relaxed, his face like a marvelous symphony."[11]

We are blessed by a God who is "abounding in love and faithfulness" (Exodus 34:6). A more literal translation of this passage could be "*huge* in love and faithfulness." God takes delight in us. This is the primary creational and anthropological affirmation within all of Scripture, and its challenge is as far-reaching as it is startling! To believe and to feel that we and our world are good; to take delight in one another and in our lives; to let the experience of delight radiate from our lives in our worship, and our work; to let delight become the essence of our witness to the world are, I believe, core practices of the living that lies before us.

Blessing is a responsibility that is particularly incumbent on us as members of a community. We are called to bless each other. Deitrich Bonhoeffer wrote that "a blessing is the visible, perceptible, effective proximity of God. A blessing demands to be passed on – it communicates itself to other people. To be blessed is to be oneself a blessing."[12]

FOR REFLECTION

Recall the definition of Sabbath as a safe place at the heart of creation. Sabbath is an environment where we are invited to practice a non-anxious presence that we may learn to live into the reality of God's essential blessing.

Sabbath practice awakens us to three things. First, we embrace the goodness of the original creation where God said it is good, very good. Do not let the doctrines of original sin or total depravity diminish the reality of original goodness. Secondly, we come to know that God experiences the same delight and pleasure in the essential nature of every person that God experienced with Jesus at his baptism when God said, "This is my beloved child in whom I take delight" (Matthew 3:17). Finally, we hear these words of blessing and delight and recognize that goodness is in all others, and we take delight in them.

There is a tightness in the world's chest, a tangled mess of stress and distraction, a constriction of the heart that blocks our ability to extend blessing. It is not through endless theological debate, not through intellectual gymnastics, or changing standards of orthodoxy that we will be set free. The heart is set free through blessing. Blessing opens the heart. It is time to untangle, loosen, and open our hearts so that we too can offer the essential blessing of God's love. Blessing begets blessing.

INTENTION ***Today I know who I really am – blessed one of God.***

BREATH PRAYER

BREATHING IN *Bless the Lord*

BREATHING OUT *oh my Soul*

DAY SEVEN

Sabbath Group

THIS WEEK WE looked at the resources we need to sustain us in our Sabbath practice – a journey of a lifetime. We learned that in freedom we can allow Sabbath to come to us. Through the soul's lament, a holy imagination, fidelity, and gratitude we discovered the essential blessing of God's love that is at the centre of all that is. We are learning that we can give ourselves up to the practice, rather than trying to control it.

OPENING PRAYER (TOGETHER)

God you are before us and behind, above and below us. You are closer to us than our closest friend. We confess that our journey is not so much about using the gifts of Sabbath for our comfort or rescue as if we could pull some blanket of peace and security over our cold and discomfited selves. It is more like caring with you, God, for the seed of eternity that is planted in our souls. But the soil of our lives is fallow and the seed so deep it struggles for light. Continue, O God, to stir the soil of our individual and communal lives that the growth that has begun in these days may continue for many, many more.

SHARING

The essential blessing at the heart of creation will be our compass
and reference point. Each person in the group is invited to share their
understanding or feelings about God's blessing as extended to them.
Let this time be free and spacious. Listen to each other with hearts of
compassion.

SING

"Take, Oh Take Me as I Am" by John L. Bell[13]

LITANY FOR CONTINUING SABBATH PRACTICE

Leader: Loving God, take, oh take me as I am.

People: These words speak to me of your acceptance, as you made me.
You know me inside out, just as I am. Here I am Lord, I offer my lament,
my fidelity, my imagination and my gratitude to you. I offer myself.

Leader: Summon out what I shall be.

People: These words speak of the potential, which is your gift to me.
What I shall be, what I could be, what you, God, are going to make of
me. I offer myself.

Leader: Set your seal upon my heart.

People: I acknowledge and cherish your blessing, oh God. I offer myself
to you and you accept me. You and I, God, are committed to each other
so that you live in me and I in you. I offer myself.

Leader: Take, oh take me as I am.

People: Summon out what I shall be. Set your seal upon my heart and
live in me.

All: Take us all this day, Lord. May we enjoy one another's company. May we make new friends. May we encourage one another. We remember our friends and colleagues who are sad or anxious today. We remember our troubled world and pray for peace and healing. We pray for ourselves, all who journey the Sabbath way with us. We thank you for your love and commitment to us; for you love the world so much that you sent us Jesus, whose we are and whom we serve. Amen.

A RITUAL OF BLESSING

Conclude with the blessing given by God to Israel in Numbers 6:23–27. Gather in a circle. Each person places their hands on or above the person next to them and says:

The Lord bless you and keep you! The Lord let his face shine upon you, and be gracious to you! The Lord look upon you kindly and give you peace!

Continue around the circle until each person has blessed every other person. The leader closes with these words:

Lord God, from the abundance of your mercy, enrich your servants and safeguard them. Strengthened by your blessing, may they always be thankful to you and bless you with unending joy. We ask this through Christ our Lord. Amen. In the name of the Father, and of the Son, and of the Holy Spirit.

Sabbath Is Celebration

My Father is working still, and I am working.

JOHN 5:17

W EEK SEVEN IS by no means the last stop on the Sabbath journey. This week, we look back and reflect on our experiences of the past six weeks while at the same time looking forward to many moments of Sabbath joy.

SABBATH PUNCTUATION

Never put a period
or colon or even a comma
where God puts a semicolon.

Unlike the
settled-before-its-time
period

or the
see-all-possibilities
colon

or the
screaming-insistently-final
exclamation point

or even the
lighthearted-Sabbath-pause
comma

the outrageous
semicolon holds
us in the middle

without yielding to one
thing or the other.
It's so easy to get lost

along the way where
there is so much
pushing and pulling.

God I believe;
Help my unbelief.
Amen; Life.

DAY 1

Beginning

Life is short and we do not have too much time to gladden the hearts of those who travel with us, so be swift to love and make haste to be kind.

HENRI FREDERIC AMIEL[1]

I HEARD TODAY FROM a young friend who is struggling to find her path in life. As she explained the difficult circumstances and challenges that she faced, she said through the tears, "I'm 23 and I'm not where I thought I would be."

We've all been there. We have our lives pretty well mapped out and we become angry and frustrated when we feel like we've lost our way or are not where "we're supposed to be." I wanted to tell her to relax; after all, she's only 23 and has her whole life in front of her. Instead, I listened to her struggle and it struck a familiar note in my own heart.

Perhaps we feel some disappointment or disorientation around our own Sabbath practice. We've been travelling this road for six weeks yet wonder where it has really led us. We may ask if we are any closer to God than we were at the beginning of this journey. At this point, apathy can seep into our lives and draw us even farther into a sense of lostness.

When we first took up Sabbath practice, there was an invitation to hold lightly our expectations for growth and change, since our performance-oriented culture tempts us to measure ourselves by some external pressure or norm. Perhaps there has been a space formed in you where you can rest. It is a place of acceptance and freshness. It is a safe place where you can be where you are without judgment. There is no final exam awaiting you at the end of the Sabbath journey. In fact, there is no end – only a holding environment that is a place of authentic and lasting change. As you experience the life, love, and truth of the Sabbath place and yearn for more, don't try to make it happen. It will come when you are open. Don't try to hold on to it. It is always there when you open to it.

FOR REFLECTION

Allow your soul's desire for God to draw you deeper into the practice. Mechthild of Magdeburg describes the human and divine perspectives of this longing. She hears the soul speak to God in these words:

> *God, you are my lover,*
> *My longing,*
> *My flowing stream,*
> *My sun,*
> *And I am your reflection.*

This is how God answers the soul:

It is my nature that makes me love you often,
For I am love itself.
It is my longing that makes me love you intensely,
For I yearn to be loved from the heart.
It is my eternity that makes me love you long,
For I have no end.[2]

As we come near to the end of this book, we know there is continuing opportunity for growth. Receive this blessing.

May the ache fall from your lips
as gently as autumn
leaves from branches.

May it flow from your heart
as naturally as water flows over stones
smoothing hard resistances.

May it be pulled easily
from pen to paper by
gravity's centering force.

May it find a place to rest
in the space between us so that we
both can be truly alive.

May it become a wise
companion
pointing the way home.

INTENTION **Today I cherish the new beginnings that come to me with each breath.**

BREATH PRAYER

BREATHING IN *God you are my lover*

BREATHING OUT *and I am your reflection*

DAY 2

Spaciousness

*Listen: there was once a king sitting on his throne.
Around Him stood great and wonderfully beautiful
columns ornamented with ivory, bearing the banners
of the king with great honor. Then it pleased the king
to raise a small feather from the ground, and he
commanded it to fly. The feather flew, not because
of anything in itself but because the air bore it along.
Thus am I, a feather on the breath of God.*

HILDEGARD VON BINGEN[3]

AS I WRITE this October morning, the leaves are letting go of the branches and falling gently to the earth, carried on the currents of air. I am reminded that there is a certain yielding in all of nature as the earth moves through its seasons. In our Sabbath practice, we too can let ourselves let go and be carried by the breath of God.

Imagine being a leaf fluttering along the path, caught by the breeze, held, blown again, yielding to the breath of God. Feel the lightness of being, the freedom from self-assertion and willful obsession, the freedom from wishing and wanting. Float, like Hildegard's feather, on the breath of God.

FOR REFLECTION

Psalm 18 is full of vivid images. Be present to this Psalm and feel the contrast between verses 1–6 and 31–36.

VERSES 1–6

I love you, O Lord, my strength. The Lord is my rock, my fortress, and my deliverer, my God, my rock in whom I take refuge, my shield, and the horn of my salvation, my stronghold. I call upon the Lord, who is worthy to be praised; so I shall be saved from my enemies. The cords of death encompassed me; the torrents of perdition assailed me; the cords of Sheol entangled me; the snares of death confronted me. In my distress I called upon the Lord; to my God I cried for help. From his temple he heard my voice, and my cry to him reached his ears.

VERSES 31–36

For who is God except the Lord? And who is a rock besides our God? – the God who girded me with strength, and made my way safe. He made my feet like the feet of a deer, and set me secure on the heights. He trains my hands for war, so that my arms can bend a bow of bronze. You have given me the shield of your salvation, and your right hand has supported me; your help has made me great. You gave me a wide place for my steps under me, and my feet did not slip.

How would you describe your relationship with God currently? Is it spacious? Is it confined?

What are the circumstances, feelings, and thoughts that accompany the state you are in?

How is God broadening the path beneath your feet?

He also allured you out of distress into a broad place
where there was no constraint, and what was set on
your table was full of fatness.

JOB 36:16

The path opened up as it does each morning
to a broad place where there is no constraint
There my head is lifted up, my eyes opened wide
There my lungs are filled with air, my steps lightened
There the table is set full of fat things to nourish my longing
The table in the presence of "mine enemies"
They too are invited to a place at its broad boards
that groan under the weight of graceful acceptance
We laugh, we feast, we have our fill, and then return
to the narrow way, where thirst and hunger grow with each step
Such is the return of Sabbath – the taste of what is to come

INTENTION **Today I savour the broad, wide-open spaces in my life.**

BREATH PRAYER

BREATHING IN *God sets my feet*

BREATHING OUT *in wide-open spaces*

DAY 3

Blessing Separateness

*Like a city breached, without wall is one who lacks
self-control.*

PROVERBS 25:28

BECAUSE WE ARE made in the image of God, there is something very deep and very powerful in us that doesn't want to be walled in. We want to love everyone; we want to experience everything.

Our scriptures begin with the affirmation that what's deepest in us, what defines us, is the *imago Dei*, the image and likeness of God. To be in the "image and likeness" of God, however, does not mean that we have stamped, somewhere in our souls, a beautiful icon. God, scripture tells us, is fire, wild, holy, undomesticated. To be in the image and likeness of God is to have this wildness in us.[4]

The separate space created by Sabbath practice offers an opportunity to direct that wild energy so that it leads us to life and not to death, to integration rather than disintegration. When we pause for breath along the Sabbath path we give the fire within a chance to reconnect to its source, God. As Rolheiser asserts,

> Anyone who tries to handle this energy without referring it to a world beyond our own will find that, far from being a source of wonder and enchantment, this fire will be a source for destruction, restlessness, and depression. Why? Precisely because this innate wildness over-charges us for life in this world. Divine fire trying to satiate itself solely within a finite situation, perhaps more clearly than anything else, explains why things don't happen smoothly in our lives. Whenever the godly energies in us are not somehow related to God, one of the following invariably results: destructive grandiosity, numbing depression, frustrating restlessness, helpless addiction, or heartless ideology.[5]

When we stand back from the *chronos* of our lives and enter into the *kairos* of the separate Sabbath space we refer the fire in our lives to its source. Our longing finds its home in God. Our restlessness is soothed in God's embrace. Our brokenness begets wholeness.

FOR REFLECTION

Consider the story of Shadrach, Meshach and Abednego in Daniel 3.

> Then King Nebuchadnezzar was astonished and rose up quickly. He said to his counsellors, "Was it not three men that we threw bound into the fire?" They answered the king, "True, O king." He replied, "But I see four men unbound, walking in the middle of the fire, and they are not hurt; and the fourth has the appearance of a god."

INTENTION **Today I enter the Sabbath space where my life returns to God.**

BREATH PRAYER

BREATHING IN *The God we serve*

BREATHING OUT *is able to save us*

DANIEL 3:17

DAY 4

Simplicity

*When I was a child, I spoke like a child, I thought
like a child, I reasoned like a child; when I became an
adult, I put an end to childish ways. For now we see in
a mirror, dimly, but then we will see face to face. Now
I know only in part; then I will know fully, even as I
have been fully known. And now faith, hope, and love
abide, these three; and the greatest of these is love.*

1 CORINTHIANS 13:11–13

THESE VERSES HAVE surfaced in my prayer over and over again
in the past few years. Sabbath, as we have learned, is a place of
growth toward God. I remember a song of my youth that claimed
that if we turned our eyes upon Jesus and looked fully at him, earthly
things would grow dim in the light of God's glory and grace.[6] However,
I have experienced quite the opposite. As I have turned my eyes to Jesus
during Sabbath pause, the things of this world have taken on sharpness
and a clarity that I have not sensed before. Sabbath practice provides
the corrective lenses through which life in all its radiance and beauty
becomes increasingly clear. I have less need to clutter my life with things
and over-activity. Now that I can see where I am going, I can choose
those things and activities that bring me closer to God and reflect my
true longing and vocation. Enough said.

For Reflection

BY GRACE

*It is by Grace we have been
saved and not by doing
so that no ego can boast.*

*The ego simply has
no ground on which
to stake a claim.*

*No idea can claim Truth.
No orthodoxy can
define the Path.*

*No experience
sublime or painful
is permanent.*

*Only Grace, that river of
life that so wants to carry us into
the future, can heal.*

*Only Grace, that solvent of love
that would dissolve all barriers,
can apply the salve to our brokenness.*

*Only Grace, whose poetry whispers
groans beyond our knowing,
can point the way.*

And Grace is here – Oh Yes! –
just below our feet
like a flowing river.

And in the Sabbath pause
we rest in her currents
and know it is true, amazing as it is.

'Tis Grace that brought
us safe thus far
and Grace will lead us home.

What <u>one</u> word brings you joy today?

How can you share that word with others?

What <u>one</u> thing is beautiful in your life today?

How can you share that beauty with others?

INTENTION **Today I need only to be held by God.**

Breath Prayer

BREATHING IN *Where God leads*

BREATHING OUT *I will follow*

DAY 5

Sacred

. . .a king who made a bridal chamber, which he plastered, painted and adorned; now what did the bridal chamber lack? A bride to enter it. Similarly, what did the universe still lack? The Sabbath. Imagine a King who made a ring. What did it lack, a signet. Similarly, what did the universe lack? The Sabbath.

ABRAHAM HESCHEL[7]

TIME SPENT PRACTICING Sabbath is time spent away from our ordinary activities. It is a time when the heart awakens to the real. As we explore Sabbath we usually sense an essential loneliness. It is not Sabbath that is the root of our loneliness. Rather, it is the increasing awareness that we are not at home in this world. The longing for more of God is the root of our loneliness. When we stop and breathe the Sabbath air we make ourselves ready for God to enter more fully into our lives.

Jesus' parable of the ten virgins in Matthew 25 points out that humans need to be aware of God's presence. (See Mark 13:33–37 and Luke 12:35–38 for other parables that call for watchfulness.)

Then the kingdom of heaven will be like this. Ten bridesmaids took their lamps and went to meet the bridegroom. Five of them were foolish, and five were wise. When the foolish took their lamps, they took no oil with them; but the wise took flasks of oil with their lamps. As the bridegroom was delayed, all of them became drowsy and slept. But at midnight there was a shout, "Look! Here is the bridegroom! Come out to meet him." Then all those bridesmaids got up and trimmed their lamps. The foolish said to the wise, "Give us some of your oil, for our lamps are going out." But the wise replied, "No! there will not be enough for you and for us; you had better go to the dealers and buy some for yourselves." And while they went to buy it, the bridegroom came, and those who were ready went with him into the wedding banquet; and the door was shut. Later the other bridesmaids came also, saying, "Lord, lord, open to us." But he replied, "Truly I tell you, I do not know you." Keep awake therefore, for you know neither the day nor the hour.

If we do not practice awareness of God present and active in all of life and longing for the divine human relationship, we may be like the five virgins who were not prepared for the bridegroom. We may be so preoccupied with the many things that demand our attention that there is little time left to become attuned to the presence of the Holy in our lives. Particularly in the postmodern context, it is easy to become so consumed with the demands of life that we actually become spiritually anesthetized.

It is not hyper-vigilance or a frantic search for God that is proposed in the Matthean parable. The virgins' problem is not that they fell asleep. The difference between the wise and the foolish virgins is that some were ready, some were not. The key is readiness. Sabbath practice does not remove one from all the regular activities of life or remove one from the challenges inherent in the postmodern world. Rather, the regular and rhythmic practice of Sabbath provides transformative occasions of greater awareness of God's presence. Regular Sabbath practice can help ready a person for the coming of the Bridegroom who seeks out the bride.

FOR REFLECTION

The practice of Sabbath is in the context of a covenantal relationship whereby time is made holy.

> There are two aspects to the Sabbath. The Sabbath is meaningful; to man and is meaningful to God. It stands in a relation to both and is a sign of the covenant entered into by both. What is the sign? God has sanctified the day, and man must again and again sanctify the day, illumine the day with the light of his soul. The Sabbath is holy by the grace of God, and is still in need of all the holiness which man may lend to it.[8]

TAKING TIME FOR SACRED FRIENDSHIP

The time has come
For us to lay down
Our weapons of
Hostility

Time to lay down
The loaded gun
Of dogma with
Its bullets of certainty

Time to disarm
The incendiary bombs
Of pragmatism that
Consumes the other

Time to sheathe
The two-edged dagger
Of particularity
That has left us both bleeding

Time to surrender the smooth stones
Of desire that have slain
Giants from the deadly slingshot of
Convincing, consuming, helping, fixing

Now in the sweet surrender
There is a space where
I can find me in you
You in me

And us in God

INTENTION **Today I welcome the Sabbath Bride.**

BREATH PRAYER

BREATHING IN *Wait for God*

BREATHING OUT *God is always near*

DAY 6

The Continuing Journey

If a man does not keep pace with his companions,
perhaps it is because he hears a different drummer.
Let him step to the music he hears, however
measured or far away.

HENRY DAVID THOREAU[9]

Every act done in the sunlight of awareness
becomes sacred.

THICH NHAT HANH[10]

KARL RAHNER USES the phrase "holy or ineffable mystery"[11] to describe an infinite, and ultimately indefinable and ineffable God. It (holy mystery) is prior, essential, and original. It is horizon and foundation of all meaning, but it cannot be fully grasped. God is called "holy" because God is the ground of our freedom, of our volition and of love.

"At the heart of every story is Mystery. The reasons we attribute to events may be far different from their true cause. Often our first interpretation of events is quite different from our last reading of them. Mystery is a process, and so is our understanding of it."[12] The continuing Sabbath journey is a journey into the mystery of God. "All the great spiritual leaders in history were people of hope. Abraham, Moses, Ruth, Mary, Jesus, Rumi, Gandhi, and Dorothy Day all lived with a promise in their hearts that guided them toward the future without the need to know exactly what it would look like. Let's live with hope."[13]

FOR REFLECTION

Not knowing where the Sabbath journey will lead can either be a source of great joy and comfort or restlessness and fear. It all depends on who you know. There is something of Thomas in all of us who long to know what lies ahead.

> Thomas said to him, "Lord, we don't know where you are going, so how can we know the way?" Jesus answered, "I am the way and the truth and the life. No one comes to the Father except through me. If you really knew me, you would know my Father as well. From now on, you do know him and have seen him" (John 14).

A FAR-OFF COUNTRY

You have followed the Sabbath path deep into the heart of
a far-off country.
In this country there is time enough to love.
In this country there is no hurry.
In this country there is no need for more.
In this country everyone is awake.
In this country all roads lead to God's heart.
The only map of this place is in your heart.
The land is the boundary line of our landscape.
The end point of our line of sight.
In this country giving is no burden.
This country is warmly familiar because it is from whence you came.
It opens to vistas of hope and peace and love.
You are a citizen of this country because you are a child of God.
This country is Sabbath
And it is nearer than you first thought.

INTENTION **Today I trust the Mystery to lead me home.**

BREATH PRAYER

BREATHING IN **One step**

BREATHING OUT **enough for me**

Blessing Each Other — A Group Celebration

Another practice invites us to bless strangers quietly, secretly. Offer it to people you notice on the street, in the market, on the bus. "May you be happy. May you be at peace." Feel the blessing move through your body as you offer it. Notice how you both receive some benefit from the blessing. Gently, almost without effort, each and every blessing becomes a Sabbath.

WAYNE MULLER[14]

The Sabbath was given only for pleasure.

HIYYA BEN ABBA[15]

EACH SABBATH GROUP will find a celebration that is authentic to them. I offer some simple questions to help you create a joyful and meaningful time together. Think outside the box.

What colours should be included in our celebration?

What elements shall we use (water, fire, earth, wind)?

What movements will help us to celebrate and remember our time together?

What do we want to say to each other?

What do we want to say to God?

What can be expressed in laughter?

What is best expressed with tears?

Finally, where do we go from here as a group?

The Lord bless you and keep you;
The Lord make his face shine upon you and be
gracious to you;
The Lord turn his face toward you
and give you peace.

NUMBERS 6:24–26

Shabbat Shalom!

ENDNOTES

Introduction

1 Abraham Joshua Heschel, *The Sabbath: Its Meaning for Modern Man*, Expanded ed. (New York: Farrar, Straus and Young, 1951), 17.

2 Ibid., 7.

3 Thomas Merton, *The Climate of Monastic Prayer*, Cistercian Studies Series. No.1. (Spencer, Mass: Cistercian Publications, 1969), 52, 53.

4 Ephesians 2:19, 20: "So then ye are no more strangers and sojourners, but ye are fellow-citizens with the saints, and of the household of God, being built upon the foundation of the apostles and prophets, Christ Jesus himself being the chief cornerstone."

Prepare

1 *Writing the Sacred: A Psalm inspired path to appreciating and writing sacred poetry* by Ray McGinnis is an excellent resource for those wishing to deepen their spiritual awareness through writing. Published by Wood Lake Publishing and available at www.woodlakebooks.com.

Week 1

1 Thomas Merton, *Conjectures of a Guilty Bystander* (New York: Doubleday and Company, 1966) p. 30.

2 Michael Casey, *Toward God: The Ancient Wisdom of Western Prayer*, First U.S. edition. ed. (Liguori, MO: Triumph Books, 1996), 24.

3 Gabriele Uhlein, *Meditations with Hildegard of Bingen* (Bear & Company, 1983), 61.

4 Heschel, 10.

5 Ibid., 11.

6 *Graffiti on a New York Subway Wall*. Reported in conversation with Bill Carter.

7 Wayne Kritsberg, John H. Lee, and Shepherd Bliss, *A Quiet Strength: Meditations on the Masculine Soul* (New York: Bantam Books, 1994), 110.

8 Heschel, 11.

9 Thomas Merton, *Wisdom of the Desert: Sayings from the Desert Fathers of the Fourth Century* (New York: New Directions Publishing Corporation, 1960), 50.

10 Kathleen Norris, *Amazing Grace: A Vocabulary of Faith* (New York: Riverhead Books, 1998), 69, 70.

11 Communauté de Taizé, *Songs and Prayers from Taizé* (Chicago, IL: GIA Publications Inc., 1991), 38.

Week 2

1 Dietrich Bonhoeffer and Eberhard Bethge, *Letters and Papers from Prison*, Enlarged ed. (London: SCM Press, 1971), 3.

2 Emory University, Division of Educational Studies, (http://www.des.emory.edu/mfp/jamessaid.html), accessed June 2003.

3 C. S. Lewis, *The Last Battle, His Tales of Narnia* (London: The Bodley Head, 1956), 224.

4   Gerald G. May, *The Awakened Heart: Living Beyond Addiction*, 1st ed. (San Francisco: HarperSanFrancisco, 1991), 97.

5   Frederick Buechner, *Telling Secrets* (San Francisco: HarperSanFrancisco, 1991), 41–52.

6   Howard L. Rice, *Reformed Spirituality: An Introduction for Believers*, 1st ed. (Louisville, Ky.: Westminster/John Knox Press, 1991), 46.

7   Paul Tillich, *The Shaking of the Foundations* (New York: C. Scribner's Sons, 1948), 162.

8   *The Presbyterian Hymnal: Hymns, Psalms, and Spiritual Songs*, 322.

Week 3

1   Heschel, 49.

2   Ibid., 3.

3   Sam Keen, *Fire in the Belly: On Being a Man* (New York: Bantam Books, 1991), 55.

4   Annie Dillard, *Pilgrim at Tinker Creek*, 1st Perennial classics ed. (New York: HarperPerennial, 1998), 9.

5   Laurent A. Daloz et al, *Common Fire: Leading Lives of Commitment in a Complex World* (Boston: Beacon Press, 1996), 121.

6   Dictionary.com, (http://dictionary.reference.com/search?q=distract), accessed September 2003.

7   John Donne, *John Carey, and John Donne, Major Works* (Oxford; New York: Oxford University Press, 2000), 373.

8   Helen Keller, *Helen Keller's Journal* (Bath: Cedric Chivers, 1973), 35.

9   May, 45.

10 Ibid., 49.

11 *James Holmes Quotes*, (http://www.jamesholmes.com/quotes.html), Accessed, March 2003.

12 Heschel, 4.

13 Rainer Maria Rilke and John J. L. Mood, *Rilke on Love and Other Difficulties. Translations and Considerations of Rainer Maria Rilke*, 1st ed. (New York: Norton, 1975), 28.

14 *The Presbyterian Hymnal: Hymns, Psalms, and Spiritual Songs*, 404.

15 Ibid.

Week 4

1   *Coalition on Homelessness*, San Francisco, (http://www.sf-homlessness-coalition.org), accessed June 2001.

2   Max De Pree, *Leadership Is an Art* (New York: Currency, 2004), 22.

3   Casey, 28.

4   Ann Belford Ulanov and Barry Ulanov, *Primary Speech: A Psychology of Prayer* (Atlanta, GA: J. Knox, 1982), 45.

5   Daloz, 147.

6   Everett Fox, *The Five Books of Moses: Genesis, Exodus, Leviticus, Numbers, Deuteronomy; A New Translation with Introductions, Commentary, and Notes*, The Schocken Bible Vol. 1, (New York: Schocken Books, 1995).

7   Ibid., 13.

8   Cornelius Plantinga Jr., *Not the Way It's Supposed to Be: A Breviary of Sin* (Wm. B. Eerdmans Publishing Company, (January 1995), 14.

9   *Jewish Prayer Service*, "The Living Pulpit," (Bronx, NY: Living Pulpit, Inc., 1998), 49.

10   Early Jewish Writings.com, (http://www.earlyjewishwritings.com/odessolomon.html), accessed November 2003.

11   May, 29.

12   Ibid., 29.

13   Augustine and John Kenneth Ryan, *The Confessions of St. Augustine*, 1st ed. (Garden City, NY: Image Books, 1960), 369.

14   Wayne Muller, *Sabbath: Restoring the Sacred Rhythm of Rest* (New York: Bantam Books, 1999), 179.

15   Composer unknown.

16   Augustine and Ryan, *The Confessions of St. Augustine*, 254.

17   Richard J. Foster, *Prayer: Finding the Heart's True Home*, 1st ed. ([San Francisco]: HarperSanFrancisco, 1992), 35.

Week 5

1   Heschel, epilogue.

2   Karl Barth, *Church Dogmatics*, vol. III Doctine of Creation (Edinburgh, Scotland: T & T Clark, 1958), 98.

3   Jean Pierre de Caussade, *The Sacrament of the Present Moment*, 1st Harper & Row pbk. ed. (San Francisco: Harper & Row, 1982), 81.

4   Wendy Ladd, *Six Months Later: Remembering 9/11*, Columbia Graduate School of Journalism, (http://www.jrn.columbia.edu/studentwork/deadline/2002/ladd–towers.asp), accessed March 2002.

5   Ronald Rolheiser, *The Holy Longing: The Search for a Christian Spirituality*, 1st ed. (New York: Doubleday, 1999), 216.

6   Matthew Fox, *The Reinvention of Work: A New Vision of Livelihood for Our Time*, 1st ed. ([San Francisco, Calif.]: HarperSanFrancisco, 1994)., 41.

7   WorldofQuotes.com, (http://www.worldofquotes.com/topic/Trust/1/), accessed June 2003.

Week 6

1   Everett Fox, *The Five Books of Moses: Genesis, Exodus, Leviticus, Numbers, Deuteronomy; A New Translation with Introductions, Commentary, and Notes*, The Schocken Bible Vol. 1, (New York: Schocken Books, 1995).

2   Ronald Rolheiser, *Against an Infinite Horizon*, (New York: The Crossroad Publishing Company, 1996), 9, 10.

3   Albert Camus, *The Fall*, 1st Vintage international ed. (New York: Vintage Books, 1991), 30.

4   Rainer Maria Rilke, Franz Xaver Kappus, and Stephen Mitchell, *Letters to a Young Poet*, 1st Vintage Books ed. (New York: Vintage Books, 1987), 35.

5   *Albert Einstein*, Thinkexsist.com, (http://en.thinkexist.com/quotation/knowledge_is_limited-but_imagination_encircles/340906.html), accessed July 2003.

6   Ibid., 158.

7   Ralph Waldo Emerson, *Essays* (New York: Harper Perennial, 1981), 139.

8   Gratefulness.org, (http://www.gratefulness.org/readings/whyte_dsr.htm), accessed November 2003.

9   Rilke, *Selected Poems of Rainer Maria Rilke*, 103.

10 Wikipedia, (http://en.wikipedia.org/wiki/Abraham_Joshua_Heschel), accessed August 2003.

11 Rolheiser, *The Holy Longing: The Search for a Christian Spirituality*, 68.

12 Rolheiser, *Against an Infinite Horizon*, 16.

13 John Bell, GIA Publications, (http://www.giamusic.com/sacred_music/search_details.cfm?title_id=1290), accessed November 2003.

Week 7

1   *Seeking Peace: Brain Tumor Hospice Care*, (http://www.brainhospice.com/page4a.html), accessed January 1004.

2   Fiona Bowie and others, *Beguine Spirituality: Mystical Writings of Mechthild of Magdeburg, Beatrice of Nazareth, and Hadewijch of Brabant* (New York: Crossroad, 1990), 55, 56.

3   Hildegard von Bingen, *The Society of Archbishop Justus*, (http://justus.anglican.org/resources/bio/247.html), accessed January 2004.

4   Ron Rolheiser, (http://www.ronrolheiser.com/arc010602.html), accessed January, 2002.

5   Ron Rolheiser, (http://www.ronrolheiser.com/arc010602.html), accessed January 2002.

6   Words and Tune Helen H. Lemmel, 1922, *Cyber Hymnal*, (Cyberhymnal.com), accessed May 2003.

7   Heschel, 12.

8   Heschel, 53, 54.

9   Henry David Thoreau, *Walden, or, Life in the Woods; and, On the Duty of Civil Disobedience* (New York: New American Library, 1999), 258.

10 Surya Das, *Awakening to the Sacred: Creating a Spiritual Life from Scratch*, 1st ed. (New York: Broadway Books, 1999), 165.

11 Karl Rahner and Philip Endean, *Spiritual Writings*, Modern Spiritual Masters Series (Maryknoll, N.Y.: Orbis Books, 2004), 58.

12 Rachel Naomi Remen, *Kitchen Table Wisdom: Stories That Heal* (New York: Riverhead Books, 1996), 302.

13 Henri J. M. Nouwen, *Bread for the Journey: A Day Book of Wisdom and Faith*, 1st ed. (San Francisco: Harper SanFrancisco, 1997), 17.

14 Muller, 7.

15 Hiyya Ben Abba, *Living Pulpit*, April–June 1998. vol. 7, no. 2, 34.

BIBLIOGRAPHY

Augustine, and John Kenneth Ryan. *The Confessions of St. Augustine.* 1st ed. Garden City, NY: Image Books, 1960.

Barth, Karl. *Church Dogmatics.* Vol. III, *Doctrine of Creation.* Edinburgh, Scotland: T & T Clark, 1958.

Berry, Wendell. *A Timbered Choir: The Sabbath Poems, 1979–1997.* Washington, DC: Counterpoint, 1998.

Bly, Robert. *The Soul Is Here for Its Own Joy: Sacred Poems from Many Cultures.* 1st ed. Hopewell, NJ: Ecco Press, 1995.

Bonhoeffer, Dietrich, and Eberhard Bethge. *Letters and Papers from Prison.* Enlarged ed. London: SCM Press, 1971.

Bowie, Fiona, et al. *Beguine Spirituality: Mystical Writings of Mechthild of Magdeburg, Beatrice of Nazareth, and Hadewijch of Brabant.* New York: Crossroad, 1990.

Buechner, Frederick. *Whistling in the Dark: An ABC Theologized.* 1st ed. San Francisco: Harper & Row, 1988.

——. *Telling Secrets.* San Francisco: HarperSanFrancisco, 1991.

Camus, Albert. *The Fall.* 1st Vintage international ed. New York: Vintage Books, 1991.

Casey, Michael. *Toward God: The Ancient Wisdom of Western Prayer.* First U.S. edition. ed. Liguori, MO: Triumph Books, 1996.

de Caussade, Jean Pierre. *The Sacrament of the Present Moment.* 1st Harper & Row pbk. ed. San Francisco: Harper & Row, 1982.

Communauté de Taizé. *Songs and Prayers from Taizé.* Chicago, IL: GIA Publications Inc., 1991.

Daloz, Laurent A. et al *Common Fire: Leading Lives of Commitment in a Complex World.* Boston: Beacon Press, 1996.

Das, Surya. *Awakening to the Sacred: Creating a Spiritual Life from Scratch.* 1st ed. New York: Broadway Books, 1999.

De Pree, Max. *Leadership Is an Art.* New York: Currency, 2004.

Dillard, Annie. *Pilgrim at Tinker Creek*. 1st Perennial Classics ed. New York: HarperPerennial, 1998.

Donne, John, et al. *Major Works*. Oxford; New York: Oxford University Press, 2000.

Eliot, T. S. *Collected Poems, 1909–1962*. A limited ed. The 100 Greatest Masterpieces of American Literature. Franklin Center, PA: Franklin Library, 1978.

———. *Collected Poems, 1909–1962*. New York: Harcourt, Brace, & Co., 1991.

Emerson, Ralph Waldo. *Essays*. New York: Harper Perennial, 1981.

Foster, Richard J. *Prayer: Finding the Heart's True Home*. 1st ed. San Francisco: HarperSanFrancisco, 1992.

Fox, Everett. *The Five Books of Moses: Genesis, Exodus, Leviticus, Numbers, Deuteronomy; A New Translation with Introductions, Commentary, and Notes* The Schocken Bible; Vol. 1. New York: Schocken Books, 1995.

Fox, Matthew. *The Reinvention of Work: A New Vision of Livelihood for Our Time*. 1st ed. San Francisco: HarperSanFrancisco, 1994.

Frost, Robert, and Edward Connery Lathem. *The Poetry of Robert Frost: The Collected Poems*. 1st Owl Books ed. New York: Henry Holt, 1979.

Heidegger, Martin. *Being and Time*. London: SCM Press, 1962.

Heschel, Abraham Joshua. *The Sabbath: Its Meaning for Modern Man*. Expanded ed. New York: Farrar, Straus and Young, 1951.

Jones, Alexander ed. *The Jerusalem Bible*. Garden City, N.Y: Doubleday, 1966.

Julian, Edmund Colledge, and James Walsh. *Showings*: *The Classics of Western Spirituality*. New York: Paulist Press, 1978.

Keen, Sam. *Fire in the Belly: On Being a Man*. New York: Bantam Books, 1991.

Keller, Helen. *Helen Keller's Journal*. Bath: Cedric Chivers, 1973.

Kritsberg, Wayne, John H. Lee, and Shepherd Bliss. *A Quiet Strength: Meditations on the Masculine Soul*. New York: Bantam Books, 1994.

Lewis, C. S. *The Chronicles of Narnia: The Last Battle*. London: The Bodley Head, 1956.

"The Living Pulpit." Volume 7, Bronx, NY: Living Pulpit, Inc., 1998.

Loder, Ted. *Guerrillas of Grace*. San Diego: LuraMedia, 1984.

————. *My Heart in My Mouth: Prayers for Our Lives*. Philadelphia, PA: Innisfree Press, 2000.

May, Gerald G. *The Awakened Heart: Living Beyond Addiction*. 1st ed. San Francisco: HarperSanFrancisco, 1991.

Muller, Wayne. *Sabbath: Restoring the Sacred Rhythm of Rest*. New York: Bantam Books, 1999.

The New Interpreter's Bible: General Articles & Introduction, Commentary, & Reflections for Each Book of the Bible, Including the Apocryphal/ Deuterocanonical Books. 13 vols. Nashville: Abingdon Press, 1994.

Norris, Kathleen. *Amazing Grace: A Vocabulary of Faith*. New York: Riverhead Books, 1998.

Nouwen, Henri J. M. *Bread for the Journey: A Day Book of Wisdom and Faith*. 1st ed. San Francisco: HarperSanFrancisco, 1997.

O'Donohue, John. *Anam Cara: A Book of Celtic Wisdom*. 1st ed. New York: Cliff Street Books, 1997.

Plantinga, Cornelius Jr. *Not the Way It's Supposed to Be: A Breviary of Sin*: Grand Rapids, MI: Wm. B. Eerdmans Publishing Company, 1995.

The Presbyterian Hymnal: Hymns, Psalms, and Spiritual Songs. Large print ed. Louisville, KY: Westminster John Knox Press, 1990.

Rahner, Karl, and Philip Endean. *Spiritual Writings* Modern Spiritual Masters Series. Maryknoll, NY: Orbis Books, 2004.

Remen, Rachel Naomi. *Kitchen Table Wisdom: Stories That Heal*. New York: Riverhead Books, 1996.

Rice, Howard L. *Reformed Spirituality: An Introduction for Believers*. 1st ed. Louisville, KY: Westminster John Knox Press, 1991.

Rilke, Rainer Maria, et al. *Rilke's Book of Hours: Love Poems to God*. New York: Riverhead Books, 1996.

Rilke, Rainer Maria, et al. *Letters to a Young Poet.* 1st Vintage Books ed. New York: Vintage Books, 1987.

Rilke, Rainer Maria, and Robert Bly. *Selected Poems of Rainer Maria Rilke.* 1st ed. New York: Harper & Row, 1981.

Rilke, Rainer Maria, and John J. L. Mood. *Rilke on Love and Other Difficulties: Translations and Considerations of Rainer Maria Rilke.* 1st ed. New York: Norton, 1975.

Rolheiser, Ronald. *Against an Infinite Horizon.* New York: The Crossroad Publishing Company, 1996.

———. *The Holy Longing: The Search for a Christian Spirituality.* 1st ed. New York: Doubleday, 1999.

Thoreau, Henry David. *Walden, or, Life in the Woods; and, On the Duty of Civil Disobedience.* New York: New American Library, 1999.

Tillich, Paul. *The Shaking of the Foundations.* New York: C. Scribner's Sons, 1948.

Ulanov, Ann Belford, and Barry Ulanov. *Primary Speech: A Psychology of Prayer.* Atlanta, GA: J. Knox, 1982.

"The Utne Reader." Minneapolis, MN: Lens Publishing Company, 1997.

Walker, Alice. *The Color Purple.* 1st Harvest ed. Orlando, Fla: Harcourt, 2003.

"Weavings." v. Nashville, TN: Upper Room, 1986.

Wiederkehr, Macrina. *Season of Your Heart: Prayers and Reflections.* Revised and expanded. ed. San Francisco: HarperSanFrancisco, 1991.